# Party Jokes

AF756422

Compiled and Modified by

**Gopi A. Tejwani**

**Books For All**

Delhi-110052

**Distributed By:**
**D K Publishers Distributors P Ltd.**
1, Ansari Road, Darya Ganj,
New Delhi-110002
Phones: 3278368, 3261465 Fax : 3264368
visit us at: www.dkpd.com
e-mail: dkpd@del3.vsnl.net.in



First Published 2000
ISBN 81-7386-232-X

**Published By:**
**Books For All**
B-2, Vardhaman Palace, Nimri Commercial Centre,
Ashok Vihar Phase-IV, Delhi-110052
Phone: 7401672, 7452453
visit us at: www.lppindia.com
e-mail: lpp@nde.vsnl.net.in

**Printed At:**
D K Fine Art Press P Ltd.
Delhi-110052



**PRINTED IN INDIA**

# Preface

The other day I was listening to a Columbus radio station. The speaker was Dr. Madan Kataria, who was visiting numerous cities in the USA from Mumbai to promote a World Laughing Day. Several years ago Dr. Kataria started Laughing Clubs in Mumbai, where groups of people would gather and spontaneously laugh together for minutes to hours at a time. On the radio Dr. Kataria stated that he started the Laughing Day because he felt laughter is of great therapeutic value, particularly in a country like India where joy and laughter are not in abundance. According to Dr. Kataria, laughter has been suppressed in India for many reasons, including the thought that it is a taboo for youngsters to laugh in front of elders because it is disrespectful. Even so, Dr. Kataria promotes the act of laughing for no particular apparent reason. Of course, one may not necessarily need a comical anecdote or joke to laugh heartily, but I believe that a joke book is of immense value in generally promoting laughter.

In addition to Dr. Kataria, I also drew inspiration for this book from Mr. Khushwant Singh. It is heart-warming to know that an 84-year-old elderly statesman and my Guru, Mr. Singh, has been promoting laughter for more than a quarter-century.

It was "Khushwant Singh's Joke Book", published first in 1987, that inspired me to compile my own joke book. The jokes I have included came from parties and e-mails from friends. Unfortunately, it was virtually impossible to trace the origins of these jokes, as typically there are multiple sources, some from well in the past. Nonetheless, when you enjoy these jokes alone or at parties please keep in mind the anonymous people who indirectly contributed to this compilation.

I have spent a considerable amount of time collecting these jokes and shaping them to suit Indian taste. They are light-hearted jokes meant for laughter only, and are not targeted at any one particular person. For convenience, the jokes are divided into seventeen different subject sections. Each joke is identified with a title, and I encourage you to remember the ones you enjoy and tell them later at parties or social gatherings. Most of the jokes are ideal for being told in a family setting, with the exception of some of the "Romance" jokes. Nearly each joke appearing in this book has been told by me in a social setting and has resulted in healthy, hearty laughter.

I am currently compiling a second edition of this book that will consist of all new jokes. If you have a joke that is not published previously and you would like to share it with others, please e-mail the joke to me at Tejwani.1@osu.edu. Please include your name and the origin of the joke, and I will gladly acknowledge your contribution in the book.

Associate Professor
Department of Pharmacology
College of Medicine and Public Health
The Ohio State University
Columbus, OH 43210-1239, USA

# About the Editor

Dr. Gopi A. Tejwani was born in Dadu, Sind, now in Pakistan, on March 1st, 1946. After the partition, his family moved to Nagpur in Maharastra. He received his undergraduate education at the College of Science, and earned the nickname "Pyasa" from his classmates. Dr. Tejwani then earned a Master's degree in Biochemistry from the Nagpur University. He received his Ph.D. degree in Biochemistry from the All-India Institute of Sciences, in New Delhi, in 1973 and subsequently traveled to the USA for postdoctoral training. Dr. Tejwani has been on the faculty of The Ohio State University in Columbus, Ohio since 1978, where he does research in neuropharmacology and teaches graduate and medical students. Dr. Tejwani has published more than 75 original research papers in biochemistry, enzymology and neuropharmacology. He has presented his research work at international meetings in more than twenty countries. He can be reached at Tejwani.1@osu.edu.

# Contents

**What is humor?**

Isn't it true that it all depends on the way you look at things? If you have love, friends, family, good humor, and a positive attitude towards life, you have everything! You can't buy any of those things, but you can have all the material possessions imaginable and if you are poor of spirit, you have nothing!

# Academia

## Aim in life

The teacher asked her elementary class what each student wanted to become when they grew up. A chorus of responses came from all over the room.

"A cricket player," "A doctor," "An astronaut," "The president," "A fireman," "A teacher," "A race car driver"

Everyone that is, except Sonny

The teacher noticed he was sitting there quiet and still. So she said to him, "Sonny, what do you want to be when you grow up?"

"Possible" Sonny replied.

"Possible?" asked the teacher.

"Yes," Sonny said. "My mom is always telling me I'm impossible. So when I get to be big, I want to be possible."

## English Well-Spoken Here

The following signs written in English in countries where English is not a native language were spotted by travelers.

The sign in a Norwegian lounge reads: "Ladies are requested not to have children in the bar."

Tacked on the door of a Moscow hotel room: "If this is your first visit to the U.S.S.R., you are welcome to it."

An airline ticket office in Copenhagen reminds you: "We take your bags and send them in all directions."

In a certain African hotel you may choose between: "A room with a view on the sea or the backside of the country."

A sign on a clothing store in Brussels read: "Come inside and have a fit."

A hotel notice in Madrid informs: "If you wish disinfection enacted in your presence, please cry out for the chambermaid."

This notice was posted on a Rumanian hotel elevator: "The lift is being fixed for the next days. During that time we regret that you will be unbearable."

The room service in a Lisbon hotel tells you: "If you wish for breakfast, lift the telephone and ask for room service. This will be enough for you to bring your food up."

This sign was posted in a Scottish harbor: "For sale boat single owner green in color."

A sign at Budapest's zoo requests: "Please do not feed the animals. If you have any suitable food give it to the guard on duty."

A Polish hotel informs prospective visitors in a flyer: "As for the trout served you at the hotel Monopol, you will be singing its praise to your grandchildren as you lie on your deathbed."

A Seville tailor makes clear how he will handle commissions: "Order now your summer suit. Because is big rush we will execute customers in strict rotation"

A dentist's doorway in Istanbul proclaims:

"American dentist, 2th floor. Teeth extracted by latest methodists."

The concierge in a Sorrento hotel lets guests know he's on the job: "Contact the concierge immediately for informations. Please don't wait last minutes then it will be too late to arrange any inconveniences."

Some German hospitals now display the sign: "No children allowed in the maternity wards."

The sign at the concierge's desk in an Athens hotel reads: "If you consider our help impolite, you should see the manager."

A sign in a Hong Kong hotel warns: "Is forbidden to steal hotel towels. Please if you are not person to do such is please not to read notice."

Visitors in Czechoslovakia are invited by the tourist agency to: Take one of our horse-driven city tours - we guarantee no miscarriages."

A Rome laundry suggests: "Ladies, leave your clothes here and spend the afternoon having a good time."

A London eatery advertised for help this way: "Wanted man to wash dishes and two waitresses."

A notice in a Vienna hotel urges: "In case of fire do your utmost to alarm the hall porter."

## Computer

A man who had previously been a sailor, and was now an "academic" was very aware that ships are addressed as "she" and "her." He often wondered what gender computers should be addressed.

To answer that question, he set up two groups of computer experts. The first was composed of women, and the second of men.

Each group was asked to recommend whether computers should be referred to in the feminine gender, or the masculine gender. They were asked to give reasons for their recommendation.

**The group of women reported that the computers should be referred to in the masculine gender because:**

1. In order to get their attention, you have to turn them on.

2. They have a lot of data, but are still clueless.

3. They are supposed to help you solve problems, but half the time they are the problem.

4. As soon as you commit to one, you realize that, if you had waited a little longer you could have had a better model.

**The men, on the other hand, concluded that computers should be referred to in the feminine gender because:**

1. No one but the Creator understands their internal logic.

2. The native language they use to communicate with other computers is incomprehensible to everyone else.

3. Even your smallest mistakes are stored in long-term memory for later retrieval.

4. As soon as you make a commitment to one, you find yourself spending half

your paycheck on accessories for it.

## God and Professor

A college student was in a philosophy class which had a discussion about God's existence. The professor presented the following logic:

"Has anyone in this class heard God?" Nobody spoke.

"Has anyone in this class touched God?" Again, nobody spoke

"Has anyone in this class seen God?" When nobody spoke for the third time,

he simply stated, "Then there is no God."

One student thought for a second, and then asked for permission to reply.

Curious to hear this bold student's response, the professor granted it, and the student stood up and asked the following questions of his classmates:

"Has anyone in this class heard our professor's brain?" Silence.

"Has anyone in this class touched our professor's brain?" Again, silence.

"Has anyone in this class seen our professor's brain?"

When nobody in the class dared to speak, the student concluded, "Then, according to our professor's logic, it must be true that our professor has no brain!"

## How old are dinosaurs?

Some tourists in the Chicago Museum of Natural History were marveling at the dinosaur bones. One of them asked the guard, "Can you tell me how old the dinosaur bones are?" The guard replied, "They are three million, four years, and six months old."

"That's an awfully exact number," said the tourist. "How do you know their age so precisely?"

The guard answered, "Well, the dinosaur bones were three million years old when I started working here, and that was four and a half years ago."

## Two fingers

On the first day of school, the Kindergarten teacher said, "If anyone has to go to the bathroom, hold up two fingers."

A little voice from the back of the room asked, "How will that help?"

## Two professors

One day a professor while walking on a very narrow street faced a rival coming from the opposite side whom he did not like. The street was too narrow for two to pass. The rival, pulling himself up to his full height, said haughtily: "I never make way for fools!" Smiling, the professor stepped aside and said: "I always do."

## Small boots

It was the usual muddy day in the countryside in Simla. Our first grade teacher, Miss Bhatia, had just finished putting the 36th boot on the 18th pair of little feet and was anxious to finish the last pair so she could go to lunch.

The last pair of boots was for little Sonnu Nigam, a quiet boy. Miss Bhatia had a very difficult time getting his boots on as they were a bit too small for his growing feet, but she finally won the battle.

To her dismay, little Johnny looked blandly up into her face and announced, "Teacher, these boots aren't mine." In a hurry, but wanting to be kind, Miss Bhatia groaned, but with grim gentleness removed the boots and straightened her aching back. Whereupon Johnny continued, "They're my little brother's, but Mommy said I could wear them to school today."

## Spell Backwards

Ever wonder about those people who spend Rs.20 a throw on those little bottles of Evian water? Try spelling Evian backwards.

There are only two words in the English language that spell the same object both forward and backward. They are "race car."

## Richer than Birla

One primary teacher from Rampur was visiting New Delhi and was admiring Birla Mandir. He commented that if God gave him all the wealth of Birla he will be even more rich than Birla himself. Hearing that his friend, who was also visiting with him asked, how it was possible that after acquiring all the wealth of Birla, the teacher will be even more rich than Birla? To that the teacher replied . . . "because I will continue doing tuition of my students."

## Longest words in English

As I am sure you are all aware that for years the longest word in the English language has been regarded as **antidisestablishmentarianism**

(28 letters), as found in the Oxford English Dictionary, I want to correct that perception. It has recently come to my attention that it is not the longest word.

Try these on for size: **Floccipaucinihilipilification**

(29 letters, to estimate something as worthless; used in 1741 by Sir Walter Scott)

**Interdenominalationalistically** (30 letters, relations between denominations)

**Praetertranssubstantiationalistically** (37 letters, used in 1963 by author Mark Shane in "Untimely Ripped")

**Pneumonoultramicroscopicsilicovolcanoconiosis** (45 letters, in Webster's Third International Dictionary-a coal miner's lung disease)

And finally, the big daddy of them all:

**Aequeosalinocalcalinoceraceoaluminosocupreovitriolic** (52 letters, by Dr. Edward Strother to describe the spa waters at Bristol, England)

## Two poets

Two people were strolling and talking to each other near the bank of Gomati River in Lucknow. All of suddenly, one guy started running and other guy started chasing him. An onlooker saw this and he also started running behind them. When the onlooker got hold of the second guy, he asked him why he was chasing the first guy. The second guy replied, "We both are poets. He made me listen to his poems, and now he is not listening to my poems."

## An absent-minded scientist

A well-known Indian scientist was traveling in a train. The conductor asked him for the ticket but the scientist could not find the ticket. He was looking all over but the ticket was not there. The conductor told him to forget about the ticket as he knew the scientist as one of the leading figure in India and he must have bought the ticket. The scientist while still looking for the ticket said, "You are very kind, but I must find the ticket otherwise I won't know where to get off."

## A man and a scientist

A scientist asked a man to play a game. The scientist said, "If I ask you a question and you don't the answer you pay me ten rupees. If I don't know, I pay you one hundred rupees." The man agreed. The scientist asked, "What is the distance from earth to moon?" The man did not know the answer. The scientist said it was 238,857 miles. The man gave him ten rupees.

The man asked him to tell the name of the Indian tribe whose people prefer to eat through their nose. The scientist did not know the answer and gave one hundred rupees to the man. The scientist asked the man what was the answer? The man said that he did not know the answer and gave ten rupees to the scientist.

## Three professors

Three professors (a physicist, a chemist, and a statistician) are at a meeting when a fire breaks out in a wastebasket. The physicist says, "I know what to do! We must cool down the materials until their temperature is lower than their ignition temperature and then the fire will go out."

The chemist says, "No! No! I know what to do! We must cut off the supply of oxygen so that the fire will go out due to lack of one of the reactants."

As the physicist and the chemist debate what to do, the statistician actually does something. He runs around the room lighting more fires.

The physicist and the chemist scream "What are you doing?"

The statistician replies, "We're going to need a larger sample size in order to prove your point."

## Two atoms

Two atoms walk into a bar.

First atom: "I've lost an electron!!"

Second atom: "Really? Are you sure?"

First atom: "I'm positive!"

## Being stupid

A new teacher is trying to make use of her Psychology courses. She starts her class by saying, "Everyone who thinks you're stupid, stand up."

After a few seconds, little Johnny stood up. The teacher said, "Do you think you're stupid, Johnny?"

"No, ma'am," he says, "but I hate to see you standing there all by yourself."

## Visiting Chanakya

In a classroom pupils were asked to always write in silence. One day the teacher dozed off and was awakened by some of the pupils making noise. To cover her embarrassment she said, "It was always my wish to meet the scholar Chanakya and, a while ago, I did see him in my dream."

The next day a pupil dozed off while listening to the teacher's long lecture. Upon seeing the sleeping child, the teacher woke him up and rebuked him. "Why are you sleeping during the lecture?" The pupil answered, "I also went to see the scholar Chanakya." The teacher asked, "And what did Chanakya say?", to which the pupil replied, "Chanakya said he did not meet with you yesterday."

## School is over

Mother: "Why are you home from school so early?"

Son: "I was the only one who could answer a question."

Mother: "Oh, really? What was the question?

Son: "Who threw the eraser at the principal?"

# Animals

## Peacocks

One day, a teenage girl was driving on a country road and she spotted two peacocks nearby. She put the peacocks in the backseat of the car and went to get the gas for the car. The gas station attendant asked the girl what were two peacocks doing in the car?

The girl said that she found them on a country road. Attendant said, "I think you should take them to the zoo." The girl said that it was a good idea.

Next day the girl was back to the same gas station for refill. The same attendant saw that the peacocks were still in the back seat of the car.

"Hey, they are still in the car. I thought you were going to take them to the zoo, "said the attendant.

"Oh, I did," said the girl "and we had a good time. Today I am taking them to the beach."

## Danger

Upon entering the little country store, the stranger noticed a sign saying "DANGER! " Posted on the glass door. Inside he noticed a harmless old hound dog asleep on the floor beside the cash register.

He asked the store manager, "Is THAT the dog folks are supposed to beware of?"

"Yes, that's him," he replied.

The stranger could not help but be amused. "That certainly does not look like a dangerous dog to me. Why in the world would you post that sign?"

"Because," the owner replied, "before I posted that sign, people kept tripping over him."

## Hunters

Two hunters were surprised by a large, vicious bear. Terrified, the first man begins to run but then sees that his friend is lacing up a pair of running shoes.

"Are you crazy?" cries the first man, "Those shoes won't help you outrun that bear!"

"I don't have to outrun the bear," the second man replies, "I simply have to outrun you!"

## A dead cat

A little boy is gone to school one day and while he is gone, his cat gets killed. His mother is very concerned about how he will take the news. Upon his arrival home, she explains the tragedy and tries to console the boy saying, "But don't worry, the cat is in heaven with God now."

The boy replied, "What's God going to do with a dead cat?"

## At the Zoo

A kangaroo kept getting out of his enclosure at the zoo. Knowing that he could hop high, the zoo officials put up a ten-foot fence. He was out the next morning, just roaming around the zoo. A twenty-foot fence was put up. Again he goes out.

When the fence was forty feet high, a camel in the next enclosure asked the kangaroo,

"How high do you think, they'll go?"

The kangaroo said, "Oh, about a thousand feet, I think... unless somebody remembers to lock the gate at night!"

## Camels

A mother and baby camel are talking one day when the baby camel asks, "Mom, why have I got these huge three-toed feet?"

The mother replies, "Well son, when we trek across the desert your toes will help you to stay on top of the soft sand."

"OK," said the son.

A few minutes later the son asks, "Mom, why have I got these great long eyelashes?"

"They are there to keep the sand out of your eyes on the trips through the desert."

"Thanks Mom," replies the son.

After a short while, the son returns and asks, "Mom, why have I got these great big humps on my back?" The mother, now a little impatient with the boy replies, "They are there to help us store water for our long treks across the desert, so we can go without drinking for long periods."

"That's great Mom, so we have huge feet to stop us sinking, and long eyelashes to keep the sand from our eyes and these humps to store water, but Mom..."

"Yes, son?"

"Why the heck are we in the Kolcutta zoo?"

## New Laundry Machine

An eight-year-old boy, went to pick up a very good size box of laundry detergent in a store in South Extension New Delhi. The Shopkeeper walked over, and, trying to be friendly, asked the boy if he had a lot of laundry to do.

"Oh, no laundry," the boy said, "I'm going to wash my dog."

"But you shouldn't use this to wash your dog. It's very powerful and if you wash your dog in this, he'll get sick. In fact, it might even kill him."

But the boy was not to be stopped and carried the detergent to the counter and paid for it, even as the shopkeeper still tried to talk him out of washing his dog.

About a week later the boy was back in the store to buy some candy. The shopkeeper asked the boy how his dog was doing.

"Oh, he died," the boy said.

The grocer, trying not to be an I-told-you-so, said he was sorry the dog died but added, "I tried to tell you not to use that detergent on your dog."

"Well," the boy replied, "I don't think it was the detergent that killed him."

"Oh? What was it then?"

"I think it was the spin cycle!"

## Team support

A guy was going from Amritsar to Hoshiarpur in a car. Near Dhatt village he drove his car into a ditch in a desolated area. Luckily, a local farmer came to help with his big strong horse named Rahu. He hitched Ramu up to the car and yelled, "Pull, Lalu, pull!" Ramu didn't move. Then the farmer hollered, "Pull, Babu, pull!" Ramu didn't respond.

Once more the farmer commanded, "Pull, Sonu, pull!" Nothing happened. Then the farmer nonchalantly said, "Pull, Ramu, pull!" And the horse easily dragged the car out of the ditch. The motorist was most appreciative and very curious. He asked the farmer why he called his horse by the wrong name three times. The farmer said, "Oh, Ramu is blind and if he thought he was the only one pulling, he wouldn't even try."

## Dead Dog

This guy comes home from work one day to find his beloved dog dead on the living room floor. The guy flips out, frantically trying to wake the dog up. Finally he decides to take the dog to the vet. The guy gets to the vet's office, and the vet checks the dog over. "Sir, I am sorry, but your dog is dead," the vet told the owner. The owner requests a second opinion. So the vet walks out and comes back in with a cat. The cat goes around the dog many times and sniffs the dead dog, bats at it's head, and walks away. After this, the owner finally comes to terms with his dog's death. The vet brings the owner the bill 635 Rupees. "635 Rupees!" "635 Rupees" to tell me that my dog is dead ?!?!?" the owner screams. "Well," said the vet,

"the usual exam fee is only 35 rupees, but we also had to charge you 600 rupees for the "cat scan."

## Two snakes

Two snakes were out taking a stroll when younger one turns to the other, his father, and asks:

Are we poisonous?"

"Why, do you ask? Yes we are", says the father. Again the son asks "Are you sure we're poisonous?"

"Yes we are very poisonous."

Again the son asked "Are we really really poisonous?"

"Yes we are really really poisonous. In fact we're the most

poisonous snake's in the world. Why do you ask?"

"I just bit my lip!", said the son.

## Who is the mightiest?

There was a tiger, who woke up one morning, and just felt great, he just felt so good, he went out and cornered a small monkey and roared at him: "WHO IS THE MIGHTIEST OF ALL THE JUNGLE ANIMALS?" And this poor quaking little monkey replied: "You are of course, no one is mightier than you."

A little while later this tiger confronted a deer, and just bellows out: "WHO IS THE GREATEST AND STRONGEST OF ALL THE JUNGLE ANIMALS?"

The deer is shaking so hard it can barely speak, but manages to stammer: "Oh great tiger, you are by far the mightiest animal in the jungle."

The tiger, being on a roll, swaggered, up to an elephant that was quietly munching on some weeds, and roared at the top of his voice: "WHO IS THE MIGHTIEST OF ALL THE ANIMALS IN THE JUNGLE?"

The elephant grabbed the tiger with his trunk, picked him up, slammed him down; picks him up again, and shakes him until the tiger is just a blur of orange and black, and finally throws him violently into a nearby tree.The tiger staggers to his feet and looks at the elephant and says:

"Oh ...Man, just because you don't know the answer, you don't have to get so mad."

## Cats and Dogs

What is a Cat?

1) Cats do what they want.

2) They rarely listen to you.

3) They're totally unpredictable.

4) They whine when they are not happy.

5) When you want to play, they want to be alone.

6) When you want to be alone, they want to play.

7) They expect you to cater to their every whim.

8) They're moody.

9) They leave hair everywhere.

10) They drive you nuts and cost an arm and a leg.

**Conclusion: They're tiny little women in fur coats.**

What is a Dog?

1) Dogs lie around all day, sprawled on the most comfortable piece of furniture in the house

2) They can hear a package of food opening half a block away, but don't hear you when you're in the same room.

3) They can look dumb and lovable all at the same time.

4) They growl when they're not happy.

5) When you want to play, they want to play.

6) When you want to be alone, they want to play.

7) They are great at begging.

8) They will love you forever if you rub their tummies.

9) They leave their toys everywhere.

10) They do disgusting things with their mouths and then try to give you a kiss.

**Conclusion: They're little men in fur coats**

## Two donkeys

One day on the bank of Jamuna River, two donkeys came to drink water. They had not met before. The first donkey asked the second donkey what was he doing for living? The second donkey replied that he was working with a guy who lays bricks and it was a hard job as he has to carry a heavy load all the time. The first donkey said that he was working with a dhobi and he has to carry a light load consisting of mainly dry clothes. He further said to the second donkey to join his boss as they were looking for help and it would involve only light work. The second donkey replied that he was not interested in joining dhobi. The first donkey asked why not? The second donkey who worked for a bricklayer replied, " Even though I have to work hard, I have a "bright future with my owner." How so the first donkey asked? The second donkey replied,

"My owner has a teen-age daughter who doesn't behave properly. Whenever his father gets annoyed with her, he says to her ek din tumhari shadi ek gadhe se kara dunga(One day

I am going to arrange your marriage with a donkey)."

## A learned dog

A man follows a woman out of a movie theatre, who has a dog on a leash.

He stops her and says, "I'm sorry to bother you, but I couldn't help but notice that your dog was really into the movie. He cried at the right spots, he moved nervously in his seat at the boring parts, but most of all, he laughed like crazy at the funny parts. Don't you find it unusual?"

"Yes," she replied, "I found it very unusual. He hated the book!"

## Crazy Horse

There's this guy who had been lost and walking in the hills of Himachal Pradesh for about two weeks. One day, he sees the home of a gyani. Tired and weak, he crawls up to the house and collapses on the doorstep. The gyani finds him and nurses him back to health. Feeling better, the man asks the gyani for directions to the nearest town. On his way out the backdoor, he sees this horse. He goes back into the house and asks the gyani, "Could I borrow your horse and give it back when I reach the town?" The missionary say, "Sure, but there is a special thing about this horse. You have to say "Thank God" to make it go and 'Yamraj' to make it stop."

Not paying much attention, the man says, "Sure, ok." So he gets on the horse and say, "Thank God" and the horse starts walking. Then he says, "Thank God, thank God," and the horse starts trotting. Feeling really brave, the man say, "Thank God, thank God, thank God, thank God, thank God" and the horse just takes off.

Pretty soon he sees this cliff coming up and he's doing everything he can to make the horse stop. "Whoa, stop, hold on!!!" Finally he remembers, "Yamraj!!"

The horse stops 4 inches from the cliff. The man leans back in the saddle and says, "Thank God."

horse stops coming. Feeling really bad, the man says, "Thank God, thank God, thank God, thank God, thank God!" Still the horse just takes off.

Pretty soon he sees the cliff coming up and he's done everything he can to make the horse stop. When stop, he'd [illegible] finally he remembers. "Amen!"

The horse stops inches from the cliff. The man leans back [illegible] saddle and says, "Thank God."

# Automobiles

## Trucker and three motorcyclists

One day a truck driver stopped at a truck stop to have lunch. When he was having lunch in the restaurant three motorcyclists entered there. One biker grabbed truck drivers' tandoori chicken. Another took away his nan and the third one finished his laddu. The truck driver did not say a word, paid his bill to the cashier and left.

One motorcyclist said to cashier "He isn't much of a person, is he?"

He is also not much of a driver cashier replied. He just backed his truck over three motorcycles and left.

## Peaceful demise

When I die, I want to go peacefully like my grandfather did, in his sleep...

Not screaming like the other passengers in his car.

## Crossing red ligh

Two elderly women were out driving in a large car. Both could barely see over the dashboard. As they were cruising along, they came to an intersection. The stoplight was red but they just went on through the red light.

The woman in the passenger seat thought to herself, "I must be losing my mind, I swear we just went through a red light."

After a few more minutes they came to another intersection and the light was red again, and again they went right through. This time Rajni in the passenger seat was almost sure that the light had been red, but was really concerned that she was mistaken.

She was getting nervous and decided to pay very close attention to the road and the next intersection to see what was going on.

At the next intersection, sure enough, the light was definitely red and they went right through. She turned to the woman driving and said, "Situ! Did you know we just ran through three red lights in a row?! You could have killed us!"

Situ turned to her and said, "Oh, am I driving?"

## Wrong way

As a man was driving down the freeway, his car phone rang. Answering, he heard his wife's voice urgently warning him, "Herman, I just heard on the news that there's a car going the wrong way on 280. Please be careful!"

Herman replied, "It's not just one car. It's hundreds of them!"

## Crossing red light

There are these two guys driving a car. When the guy driving blows right through the red light. "Man, you just ran that red light!", the passenger said. "Don't worry, my brother does it all the time," said the driver. Well, they continue to drive when the guy went flying through another stop light. "You ran ANOTHER stop light. You are going to get us killed!!!" exclaimed the passenger. "Don't worry, my brother does it all the time, the driver said. After a while they came to a green light when the guy stopped. "Why are you stopping?" the driver turned around and said, "Because my brother might be coming!"

He [illegible] replied, "It's not just one daddy, it's hundreds of them!"

## Crossing red light

There are these two guys driving a car. When the guy driving blows right through the red light. "Man, you just ran that red light!" the passenger said. "Don't worry, my brother does it all the time," said the driver. Well, they continue to drive when the guy went flying through another stop light. "You ran ANOTHER stop light. You are going to get us killed!!!" exclaimed the passenger. "Don't worry, my brother does it all the time," the driver said. After a while they came to a green light which the guy stopped. "Why are you stopping?" the driver turned around and said, "Because my brother might be coming!"

# Doctors

## Gravely ill

After examining a guy the doctor told his wife that he wanted to talk to her in private. She met him outside the hallway. The Doctor said, "Your husband is very sick but there are three things you can do to ensure his survival."

1. Fix him three healthful, delicious meals every day.

2. Give him a stress-free environment at home and don't complain about any thing.

3. Finally, make passionate love to him every day.

On the drive back home the guy asked his wife, what did the doctor say? I am sorry said the wife, but you are not going to make it.

## Insane Asylum

Walking past the big wooden fence around the insane asylum, a doctor hears everyone inside chanting, "Thirteen! Thirteen! Thirteen!"

His curiosity piqued, he finds a hole in the fence and looks inside.

All of a sudden a finger shoots through the hole and pokes out his eye, and the inmates start wildly chanting, "Fourteen! Fourteen! Fourteen!"

## You are in my will

The patient shook his doctor's hand in gratitude and said, "Since we are the best of friends, I would not want to insult you by offering payment."

But I would like for you to know that I had mentioned you in my will.

"That is very kind of you," said the doctor emotionally, and then added, "Can I see that prescription I just gave you? I'd like to make a little change . . ."

## Two legs

An old man goes to his doctor, complaining about a pain in his leg that doesn't heal and wants a diagnosis and explanation. The doctor checks out his leg, but can't find anything wrong. So he gives the old guy a full physical exam, and still can't come up with any possible explanation for the pain. The doctor hands the patient his bill and says, "I'm sorry but the pain in your leg is simply caused by old age, there's nothing I can do about it."

The old man replies with a look of disbelief, "That's impossible! That can't be!"

The Doctor says, "What do you mean? I'm the expert here; if you know so much, how can you say it's NOT old age?"

The patient answers, "I'm no doctor but it doesn't take a medical degree to tell that your diagnosis is wrong. Clearly you're mistaken. After all my other leg feels just fine."

"So what?" says the doctor "What difference does that make?"

"Well it doesn't hurt a bit, and it's the SAME AGE!"

## Nice containers

Lakhiram desperately wanted to become a doctor and had really crammed for his medical boards, so he wasn't in the least fazed by the question: "Name the three advantages of breast milk."

Quickly he wrote:

1. It contains the optimum balance of nutrients for the newborn child.

2. As it is contained within the mother's body, it is protected from germs and helps develop the child's immune system.

Then Lakhiram was stumped. Sitting back and racking his brain until he'd broken into a sweat, he finally scribbled:

3. It comes in such nice containers.

## I can hear you

An elderly rich gentleman had serious hearing problems for a number of years. He finally went to a doctor, and was fitted with an excellent hearing aid. He returned a month later for a checkup, and the doctor said,

"Your hearing is perfect! Your family must be really pleased that you can hear again."

The gentleman replied, "Oh, I haven't told my family yet. I just sit around and listen to the conversations. I've changed my will three times!"

## Light bulb

One psychiatrist was taking rounds of his ward when he saw one patient pretending to stitch his shirt with a finger and rope and the other patient was red faced and hanging upside down from the ceiling. The psychiatrist asked the patient on the floor what was he doing? He said he was trying to do embroidery on his shirt. He then asked what was his friend doing hanging upside down from the ceiling? He said his friend thought he was a light bulb! The psychiatrist told him to ask his friend to come down. Otherwise, he may get hurt. The patient sitting on the floor replied, "What? Do you want me to work in the dark?"

## Heavens and Earth

When a new patient settled comfortably on the couch, the psychiatrist began his therapy session. The doctor said, "I am not aware of your problem, so perhaps, you should start at very beginning."

"Of course, " replied the patient. "In the beginning, I created the Heavens and the Earth......."

## She can't hear me

A man went to the doctor and complained that his wife can't hear him.

"How bad is it?" the doctor asks.

"I have no idea," says the husband.

"Well, please test her. Stand 20 feet away from her and say something. If she doesn't hear you, get closer and say the same thing. Keep moving closer and repeating the comment until she hears you, that way we will have an idea of her range of hearing loss."

So the man goes home and sees his wife in the kitchen working.

He asks from 20 feet away: "What are we having for dinner?" No answer.

He asks from 10 feet away: "What are we having for dinner?" No answer.

He asks from 5 feet away: "What are we having for dinner?" No answer.

Finally he is standing right behind her...."What are we having for dinner?"

She turns around, looks at him and says, "For the FOURTH time I am telling you, it's RICE and FISH."

## I am Mahatma Gandhi

A boy went to visit a mental institution where his father worked. He met one patient who had just removed his pants and shirt and wore a loin cloth. He asked the man why he did that?

The man replied, "I am Mahatma Gandhi."

The boy chuckled and asked him, "Really? How do you know?"

He explained, "God told me."

Another patient behind him snapped, "I did not!"

## An artist

An artist asked the gallery owner if there had been any interest in his paintings on display.

"I have good news and bad news, " the owner replied.

"The good news is that a man enquired about your work and wondered if it would appreciate in value after your death."

"When I told him it would, he bought all fifteen of your paintings."

"That is wonderful," the artist exclaimed.

"What is the bad news?"

"The man is your doctor....."

## Being professional

A doctor and his wife were sunbathing at the Kovalam beach when a beautiful girl in a bikini passed by. The girl looked at the doctor, smiled and said in sexy voice. "Hi handsome, how are you doing, longtime no see."

"Who was that?" Asked doctors' wife.

"Er.... just a girl I met professionally," replied the doctor.

"Oh yeah?!" snarled his wife, "In whose profession? Yours or hers?"

## Two carrots

Two carrots were walking down the road when a huge truck slammed into one of them. An ambulance was called and they rushed the little fellow off the hospital where he immediately went into hours of surgery.

Finally the doctor emerged and approached the other carrot who had been anxiously awaiting in the waiting room.

"Tell me" said the other carrot, "how is he?"

The doctor replied, "He is going to live, but he will be a vegetable for the rest of his life."

## Prescription drugs

A distraught patient phoned her doctor's office. "Is it true," the woman wanted to know, "that the medication you prescribed has to be taken for the rest of my life?"

"Yes, I'm afraid so," the doctor told her.

There was a moment of silence before the woman continued, "I'm wondering, then, just how serious is my condition. This prescription is marked 'NO REFILLS'."

## Doctor cannot see you

Suffering from a bad case of the flu, a man phoned his doctor for to get an appointment.

When he was told the scheduled date of the appointment, he became outraged and bellowed, "Three weeks? The doctor can't see me for three weeks? I could well be dead by then!"

Calmly, the receptionist replied, "If so, would you have your wife call to cancel the appointment?"

## A dentist

A dentist to a patient: "Would you help me? Could you give out a few of your loudest, most painful screams?"

Patient: "Why, Doc? It isn't all that bad this time."

Dentist: "There are so many people in the waiting room right now and I don't want to miss the 5 o'clock football game."

## What is wrong with me?

A man goes to the doctor and tells him that he hasn't been feeling well. The doctor examines him, leaves the room and comes back with three different bottles of pills.

The doctor says, "Take the green pill with a big glass of water when you get up. Take the blue pill with a big glass of water after lunch. Then just before going to bed, take the red pill with another big glass of water."

Startled to be put on so much medicine the man stammers, "Jeez Doc, exactly what's my problem?"

Doctor says, "You're not drinking enough water."

# Engineers

## Great choice

Two engineering students were walking across campus when one said, "Where did you get such a great bike?"

The second engineer replied, "Well, I was walking along yesterday minding my own business when a beautiful woman rode up on this bike. She threw the bike to the ground, took off all her clothes and said,

"Take what you want.'"

The second engineer nodded approvingly,

"Good choice; her clothes probably wouldn't have fit you, anyway."

## Wife or Mistress?

An architect, an artist and an engineer were discussing whether it was better to spend time with the wife or a mistress. The architect said he enjoyed time with his wife, building a solid foundation for an enduring relationship.

The artist said he enjoyed time with his mistress, because of the passion and mystery he found there.

The engineer said, "I like both."

"Both?"

Engineer: "Yeah. If you have a wife and a mistress, they will each assume you are spending time with the other woman, and you can go to the plant and get some work done."

## An airplane and a computer

Bill Gate, the founder of Microsoft and world's richest man was testifying in front of the US Senate bragging the advances' computer industry has made in inventing new and powerful computers that cost less now than ever before. He gave this analogy:

"If the aerospace industry had made advances similar to those made by the computer industry, a Boeing 747 would cost as much as a large pizza" The CEO of the Boeing Company was also there. He snapped back, "And how would you want your airplane to crash twice a day?"

4. Comprehending Engineers(Engineers)

To the optimist, the glass is half full.

To the pessimist, the glass is half empty.

To the engineer, the glass is twice as big as it needs to be.

## The difference

What is the difference between Mechanical Engineers and Civil Engineers?

Mechanical Engineers build weapons.

Civil Engineers build targets.

## Two Engineers

Two young engineers fresh out of college put in applications for an engineering position with a company. Both clients having the exact same qualifications, they were asked to take a test by the Department manager to help decide which one to hire.

Upon completion of the test, both applicants had missed only one of the questions. After reviewing the tests, the manager decided to speak with the losing applicant first.

Manager: Thanks for your interest, but we have decided to give the position to the other applicant.

Applicant: Why would you do that? We both got nine questions correct, why choose the other applicant over me?

Manager: We have made our decision not based upon the correct answers, but on the question you missed.

Applicant: And just how would once incorrect answer be better than the other?

Manager: Simple. The other applicant answered "I don't know" for question five. Your answer was "Neither do I."

## Computer Engineer

Four men rode in a car: a mechanical engineer, an electrical engineer, a chemical engineer, and a computer engineer.

The car stalled out.

The mechanical engineer said, "It must be the pistons; let's repair them and be on our way."

The electrical engineer said, "It has to be the spark plugs; we'll replace them and be ready to roll in no time at all."

The chemical engineer said, "No, it's got to be bad gas; we'll flush the system and be on our way."

They turned to the computer engineer. "What do you think we should do?" they asked.

The computer engineer shrugged and said, "Let's get out of the car, close the doors, then get back in and try restarting it."

# Family

## Grandfather

A three-year-old girl and her grandfather were standing in front of a mirror. The girl asked her grandfather

Did God make you grandpa?

Yes, God made me, said the grandpa

Did God make me too?

Yes, he did, said the Grandpa.

After looking into a mirror for some more time the girl said

"You know Grandpa; God is doing a much better job lately."

## Fire Truck

Three children were playing when a home caught fire in their neighborhood. A fire truck came and firemen and a small dog came out of the fire truck. All the children are wondering why the dog was there?

The eldest kid said: "The dog ıs there to keep people away from the fire."

The middle kid said: "The dog is there to give firemen good luck."

The youngest kid said: "The dog is needed to find the fire hydrant."

## A mailman

One day a mailman was greeted by a five-year-old boy and a huge dog in front of a house.

The mailman asked the boy "Does your dog bite?"

No, the boy said. When the mailman went to deliver the mail, the huge dog bit him.

The mailman yelled "I thought your dog does not bite"

"He does not," replied the boy. "That is not my dog."

## Dinner

One day a lady invited some people to dinner. At the table the lady asked her five-year-old daughter "Would you like to say the prayer?"

I wouldn't know what to say, the daughter replied.

Just say what you hear mummy say, Advised father to his daughter. The daughter bowed her head and said

"Dear Lord, why on earth did I invite all these people to dinner?"

## Whisper

One day a family was playing bridge with their friends at

home when their three-year-old son said

I want to go and pee

The mother said don't say pee ....... whisper

That night the son entered in his parents bed room and was pulling his dad's arm. What do you want? Asked sleepy father

I want to whisper said the son.

Oh, all right the father said, then leave my arm alone and whisper in my ear..

## Pork Juicer

A man and his 5-year-old son, whose favorite pastime was nagging for anything and everything, were in a technology fair in Germany. The man as well his son was amazed with the technological advances of the late nineties.

They pass through a popcorn counter, and the little one starts shouting for a bag. Then they passed by a special shop selling hi-tech juicer and giving demos. The salesman was shouting, "Put the fruits in and get the juice..." They went in, the son starts crying for an orange juice. They put an orange in the machine and the orange juice came out of the machine. Then he had mango juice and melon juice. Then they come in front of a big machine, which takes in pigs and delivers 'Pork' juice from a designated outlet. The son started shouting for a 'pork' juice. Dad got him the pork juice and was surprised at his so's appetite for various juices. When the son was finished with the pork juice, he said to his father,

"Dad, what a nice machine! Is there any machine which takes in juice and delivers pigs from a designated outlet."

"Yes, of course. Your mother."

## Forks

Little Seema was mothers' big helper. She helped set the table when company was due for dinner. Presently everything was on, the guest came in, and everyone sat down. Then Mother noticed something was missing.

"Susan," she said, "You didn't put a knife and fork at your uncle's place.'

"I thought he wouldn't need them," explained Seema. "Daddy says . . . he always eats like a horse!

## Anonymous Gift

A young couple got married and went away on their honeymoon. After two weeks they came back and finally put away all of the presents they received from friends and family. Since this was a new home, the process took some time. The silver went into the closet, items were put on the walls for display and some of the more intimate apparel was put in the bedroom drawers.

A week later, they received in the mail two tickets for a popular show where tickets were impossible to get. They were very excited and warmed by the gesture of the person who sent this. Inside the envelope, however, was only a small piece of paper with a single line.

"Guess who sent them."

The couple had much fun trying to identify the donor, but failed in the effort. They went to the theater, and had a wonderful time. On their return home late at night, still trying to guess the identity of the unknown host, they found the house stripped of every article of value. And on the bare table in the dining room was a piece of paper on which was written in the same handwriting as was the enclosure with the tickets:

"Well, now you know!"

## A cemetery

A man placed some flowers on the grave of his dearly departed mother and started back toward his car when his attention was diverted to another man kneeling at a grave. The man seemed to be praying with profound intensity and kept repeating, "Why did you have to die? Why did you have to die?"

The first man approached him and said, "Sir, I don't wish to interfere with your private grief, but this demonstration of pain is more than I've ever seen before. For whom do you mourn so deeply? A child? A parent?"

The mourner took a moment to collect himself, then replied, "My wife's first husband."

## Prayer

Two young boys were spending the night at their grandparent's house. At bedtime, the two boys knelt beside their beds to say their prayers when the youngest one began praying at the top of his lungs, "I PRAY FOR A NEW BICYCLE. I PRAY FOR A NEW NINTENDO. I PRAY FOR A NEW VCR..."

His older brother leaned over and nudged the younger brother and said, "Why are you shouting your prayers? God is not hard on hearing"

To which the little brother replied, "No, but Gramma is!"

## Eating Gunpowder

A man once counseled his son that if he wanted to live a long life, the secret was to sprinkle a little gunpowder on his alu ka paratha every morning. The son did this religiously, and he lived to the age of 93. When he died, he left 14 children, 28 grandchildren, 35 great-grandchildren, and a 15-foot hole in the wall of the crematorium.

## The truth and nothing but the truth

A large family, with seven children, moved to Mumbai. They were having a difficult time finding an apartment to live in. Many apartments were large enough, but the landlords objected to the large family. After several days of searching, the father asked the mother to take the four younger children to visit the cemetery, while he took the older three to find an apartment. After they had looked most of the morning, they found a place that was just right. Then the landlord asked the usual question: "How many children do you have?" The father answered with a deep sigh, "Seven... but four are with their dear mother in the cemetery."

He got the apartment!

## How Rich Are We?

One day a father who was a rich industrialist from Chandigarh took his son to a trip to the country side in Bhatinda with the firm purpose to show him how poor people can be. They spent a day and a night in the farm of a very poor family.

When they got back from their trip, the father asked his son, "How was the trip?"

"Very good Dad!"

"Did you see how poor people can be?" the father asked.

"Yeah!"

"And what did you learn?"

The son answered, "I saw that we have a dog at home, and they have four. We have a pool that reaches to the middle of the garden; they have a creek that has no end. We have imported lamps in the garden; they have the stars. Our patio reaches to the front yard; they have a whole horizon."

When the little boy was finishing, his father was speechless.

His son added, "Thanks, Dad, for showing me how poor we are!"

## A Beautiful Story

A woman came out of her house and saw three old men with long white beards sitting in her front yard. She did not recognize them. She said "I don't think I know you, but you must be hungry. Please come in and have something to eat." Is the man of the house home?" they asked. "No," she said. "He's out."

"Then we cannot come in," they replied. In the evening when her husband came home, she told him what had happened. "Go tell them I am home and invite them in!" The woman went out and invited the men in.

"We do not go into a House together," they replied."Why is that?" she wanted to know. One of the old men explained: "His name is Wealth," he said pointing to one of his friends, and said pointing to another one,

"He is Success, and I am Love." Then he added, "Now go in and discuss with your husband which one of us you want in your home."

The woman went in and told her husband what was said. Her husband was overjoyed. "How nice!!" he said. "Since that is the case, let us invite Wealth. Let him come and fill our home with wealth!"

His wife disagreed. "My dear, why don't we invite Success?"

Their daughter-in-law was listening from the other corner of the house. She jumped in with her own suggestion: "Would it not be better to invite Love? Our home will then be filled with love!"

"Let us heed our daughter-in-law's advice," said the husband to his wife. "Go out and invite Love to be our guest."

The woman went out and asked the three old men, "Which one of you is Love? Please come in and be our guest."

Love got up and started walking toward the house. The other two also got up and followed him.

Surprised, the lady asked Wealth and Success: "I only invited Love. Why are you coming in?" The old men replied together: "If you had invited Wealth or Success, the other two of us would have stayed out, but since you invited Love, wherever He goes, we go with him. Wherever there is Love, there is also Wealth and Success!!!!!!"

## Learning

A father and son went fishing one day. After a couple hours out in the boat, the boy suddenly became curious about the world around him. He asked his father, "How does this boat float"

The father thought for a moment, then replied, "Don't rightly know, son."The boy returned to his contemplation, then turned back to his father, "How do fish breath underwater?"

Once again the father replied, "Don't rightly know, son." A little later the boy asked his father, "Why is the sky blue?" Again, the father replied, "Don't rightly know, son."

Worried he was going to annoy his father, he says, "Dad, do you mind my asking you all of these questions?"

"Of course not son. If you don't ask questions, you'll never learn anything!"

## Before You Get Married

"Honey," said a husband to his wife, "I invited a friend home for supper."

"What? Are you crazy? The house is a mess, I didn't go shopping, all the dishes are dirty, and I don't feel like cooking a fancy meal!"

"I know all that."

"Then why did you invite a friend for supper?" wife asked.

"Because the poor fool's thinking about getting married," said the husband

## A future son-in-law

Father: "I spent Rs. 45,000 on my daughter's education, and you want to marry her on your income of Rs. 14,000 a year???"

Future son-in-law: "Well... look at it this way 'Dad' - that's over a 30% annual return on your investment."

## Wedding Vows

During the wedding rehearsal, the groom approached the pastor with an unusual offer. "Look, I'll give you Rs.1000 if you'll change the wedding vows. When you get to me and the part where I am to promise to 'love, honor and obey' and 'forsaking all others, be faithful to her forever, I would appreciate it if you would just leave that part out." He passed the minister a Rs.1000 bill and walked away satisfied.

It is now the day of the wedding, and the bride and groom have moved to that part of the ceremony where the vows are exchanged.

When it comes time for the groom's vows, the pastor looks the young man in the eye and says:

"Will you promise to prostrate yourself before her, obey her every command and wish, serve her breakfast in bed every morning of your life and swear eternally before God and your lovely wife that you will not ever even look at another woman, as long as you both shall live?"

The groom gulped and looked around, and said in a tiny voice, "Yes."

At the reception, the groom leaned toward the pastor and hissed, "I thought we had a deal."

The pastor put the Rs.1000 bill into his hand and whispered back, "She made me a much better offer."

## Your Tattoo

The doctor in Tamilnadu noted with astonishment a tattoo of a peacock on the shoulder of his high society 70 year old patient, who was in his office for her annual check up. She told him that she had wanted one her whole life, so she and her 16-year-old grandson decided that they would have birthday tattoos together.

The doctor inquired why she had not got one sooner.

"Until now," she replied, "I was afraid of what my mother would say."

## Being patient

A man observed a woman in the grocery store with a three-year-old girl in her basket. As they passed the cookie section, the child asked for cookies and her mother told her "no." The little girl immediately began to whine and fuss, and the mother said quietly,

"Now Neena, we just have half of the aisles left to go through; don't be upset. It won't be long."

The man passed the Mother again in the candy aisle. Of course, the little girl began to shout for candy. When she was told she couldn't have any, she began to cry. The mother said, "There, there, Neena, don't cry. Only two more aisles to go, and then we'll be checking out."

The man again happened to be behind the pair at the checkout, where the little girl immediately began to clamor for gum and burst into a terrible tantrum upon discovering there would be no gum purchased today. The mother patiently said, "Neena, we'll be through this check out stand in five minutes, and then you can go home and have a nice nap."

The man followed them out to the parking lot and stopped the woman to compliment her. "I couldn't help noticing how patient you were with little Neena..."

The mother broke in, "My little girl's name is Dimple... I am Neena."

## Smile

A religious mother noticed that it was about time for school to dismiss and since it looked like it would rain, she drove toward the school to pick up her six-year-old daughter. She turned down the street to see her daughter running towards her down the sidewalk. A lightning bolt flashed and the little girl looked up towards the sky, smiled and then began running towards her mother's car. Another lightning bolt flashed and again the little girl looked towards the sky, smiled and resumed running. This happened several more times until the little girl finally arrived at where her mother was parked. Her mom immediately inquired as to the strange behavior. "Why did you keep stopping and smiling at the sky," she asked her daughter."

I had to, mommy. God was taking my picture."

## Twins

A census taker in a rural area went up to a farmhouse and knocked. When a woman came to the door, he asked her how many children she had and their ages. She said, "Let us see now, there's the twins,

Meena and Veena, they're eighteen. And the twins,

Sony & Bony, they're sixteen. And the twins,

Mohini and Rohini, they're fourteen—— "

"Hold on!" said the census taker, "Did you get twins every time?"

The woman answered, "Heck no, there were hundreds of times we didn't get anything'."

## Meeting a stranger

When we moved to Columbus from New Jersey, one day, I told my three-year-old son that he should not talk to strangers on the road.

My son said: why not? You can always ask their names.

## A playpen

Gomati Abhayankar was almost going crazy with her three kids. She complained to her best friend, "They're driving me nuts. Such pests, they give me no rest and I'm halfway to insanity."

"What you need is a playpen to separate the kids from yourself," her friend said.

So Gomati bought a playpen.

A few days later, her friend called to ask how things were going.

"Superb! I can't believe it," Gomati said. "I get in that pen with a good book and the kids don't bother me one bit!"

## Don't talk to me

Arjan and Aruna were married for a long time. Arjan has to work early in the morning. Since Aruna is the early riser, she used to wake Arjan up at 6:00 every morning.

One day they had argument over something and Arjan told his wife, "Don't ever talk to me again."

Next day Arjan woke up in the sofa at about 10 in morning. A slip from Aruna was lying on the coffee table saying, "Arjan, it's time to wake up."

## Big eyes

After studying in the USA, Anil Matthew went to India to get married to a girl selected by his parents. He had never seen the girl before but still got married to her. The wedding went smoothly. On the first night, his new bride came covering her head with a Ghunghat(A covering on the head). As soon as Anil removed her Ghunghat, he was taken a back. His wife had big and beautiful eyes but they were crossed(cross-eye, strabismus). But his wife was very proud of her eyes and asked Anil,

Hanji, Kahiye, meri ankhen Hema Malini ki Ankhon se milti hain ki nahin?

(Please tell me whether my eyes resemble with those of Hema Malini?)

Anil was dumbfounded and did not say any thing. His wife repeated Hanji, Kahiye, meri ankhen Hema Malini ki Ankhon se milti hain ki nahin?

(Please tell me whether my eyes resemble with those of Hema Malini?)

Anil was still very polite and did not say any thing. However, his wife was persistent and asked again

Hanji, Kahiye, meri ankhen Hema Malini ki Ankhon se milti hain ki nahin?

(Please tell me whether my eyes resemble with those of Hema Malini?)

Finally an irritated Anil replied

Aapki ankhen to ek dusre se hi nahin milti hain to Hema Malini se kya milengi?

(Your eyes don't resemble even each other, how can they resemble those of Hema Malini?

## Weighing machine

One day a guy with a big paunch was weighing himself on a bathroom scale and was compressing his tummy simultaneously. His wife commented that he was not going to weigh less by compressing his tummy! The guy replied, "No honey, if I don't compress my tummy, I cannot even see the scale!"

## Answer machine

You will listen the following message kept on the Answer Machine of my son when you call him:

Hi. This is Samir.

If you are the credit card company, I already sent the money.

If you are my parents, please send money.

If you are my friends, you owe me money.

If you are my girl friend, don't worry, I have plenty of money.

# Lawyers

## Speeding

In an Old Delhi court, a judge fined a man 1000 Rupees for speeding and gave him a receipt. What am I supposed to do with this, frame it, snapped the man sarcastically?

"No save it" Replied the judge. When you get three, you will be riding a bicycle.

## Do You Know Me?

A Nagpur prosecuting attorney called his first witness to the stand in a trial - a grand motherly, elderly woman. He approached her and asked,

"Mrs. Trivedi, do you know me?"

She responded, "Why, yes, I do know you Mr.Nanavati. I've known you since you were a young boy, and frankly, you've been a big disappointment to me. You lie, cheat on your wife, you manipulate people, and talk about them behind their backs. You think you're a rising big shot when you haven't the brains to realize you never will amount to anything more than a two-bit paper pusher. Yes, I know you."

The lawyer was stunned. Not knowing what else to do, he pointed across the room and asked, "Mrs. Trivedi, do you know the defense attorney?"

She again replied, "Why, yes I do. I've known Mr. Bradley since he was a youngster too. I used to baby-sit him for his parents. And he, too, has been a real disappointment to me."

He's lazy, bigoted, and he has a drinking problem. The man can't build a normal relationship with anyone and his law practice is one of the shoddiest in the entire state of Maharashtra. Yes, I know him."

At this point, the judge rapped the courtroom to silence, and called both counselors to the bench. In a very quiet voice, he said with menace, "If either of you asks her if she knows me, you'll be jailed for contempt of court!"

## Coming to court

Judge to a defendant: Aren't you ashamed, coming here for the third time?

Defendant: Well, you come here every day.

## Honest Lawyer

An investment counselor went out on her own. She was shrewd and diligent, so business kept coming in, and pretty soon she realized she needed an in-house counsel, so she began interviewing young lawyers.

"As I'm sure you can understand," she started off with one of the first applicants, "in a business like this, our personal integrity must be beyond question." She leaned forward. "Mr. Khosla, are you an *honest* lawyer?"

"Honest?" replied the job prospect. "Let me tell you something about being honest. Why, I'm so honest that my father lent me fifty thousand rupees for my education, and I paid back every paisa the minute I tried my very first case."

"Impressive. And what sort of case was that?"

The lawyer squirmed in his seat and admitted, "My father sued me for the money."

## Postmortem Planning

A dying rich man gathered his lawyer, doctor and clergyman at his bedside and handed each of them separately, an envelope containing Rs two lakhs in cash. He made them each promise that after his death and during his repose, they would place the three envelopes in his coffin. He told them that he wanted to have enough money to enjoy the next life or in case he is buried by mistake and wakes up in the coffin.

A week later the man died. At the wake, the lawyer and doctor and clergyman, each concealed an envelope in the coffin and bid their old client and friend farewell. When they were returning from the cemetery the clergyman, feeling guilty, blurted out a confession saying that there was only Rs one lakh in the envelope he placed in the coffin. He felt, rather than waste all the money, he would send it to a mission in Cochin. He asked for their forgiveness.

The doctor, moved by the gentle Clergyman's sincerity, confessed that he, too, had kept some of the money for a new x-ray machine at his hospital. The envelope, he admitted, had only Rs. Fifty thousands in it. He said, he too could not bring himself to waste the money so frivolously when it could be used to benefit others and he planned to donate the remaining money to a hospital in Nagpur.

By this time the lawyer was seething with self-righteous outrage. He expressed his deep disappointment in the felonious behavior of two of his oldest and most trusted friends. "I am the only one who kept his promise to our dying friend. I want you both to know that the envelope I placed in the coffin contained the full amount. Indeed, my envelope contained my personal check for the entire two lakh rupees!"

## The Missing Bull

A big-city lawyer was representing the railroad in a lawsuit filed by an old rancher. The rancher's prize bull was missing from the section through which the railroad passed. The rancher only wanted to be paid the fair value of the bull. The case was scheduled to be tried before the justice of the peace in the back room of the general store. The attorney for the railroad immediately cornered the rancher and tried to get him to settle out of court. The lawyer did his best-selling job, and finally the rancher agreed to take half of what he was asking.

After the rancher had signed the release and took the check, the young lawyer couldn't resist gloating a little over his success, telling the rancher, "You know, I hate to tell you this, old man, but I put one over on you in there. I couldn't have won the case. The engineer was asleep and the fireman was in the caboose when the train went through your ranch that morning. I didn't have one witness to put on the stand. I bluffed you!" The old rancher replied, "Well, I'll tell you, young fellow, I was a little worried about winning that case myself, because that darn bull came home this morning."

## A butcher shop

A dog ran into a butcher shop and grabbed a big chunk of meat from the counter. Fortunately, the butcher recognized the dog as belonging to his lawyer.

The butcher called his lawyer and asked, "If your dog stole a chunk of meat from my shop, would you be liable for the cost of the meat?"

The lawyer replied, "Of course, how much worth the meat was?"

The butcher said it was worth 50 rupees.

A few days later the butcher received a check in the mail for 50 rupees. Attached to it was a bill for 400 rupees for Legal Consultation Service.

## Can't speak Hindi

"Your Honor, I want to bring to your attention how unfair it is for my client to be accused of theft. He arrived in Kanpur a week ago and barely knows his way around. What's more, he only speaks a few words of Hindi."

The Judge looked at the defendant and asked, "How much Hindi can you speak?"

The defendant looked up and said, "Apna batua do"("Give me your wallet!")

# Life

## Remembering dead

After dying in a car crash, three friends go to Heaven for orientation. They are all asked the same question: "When you are in your casket, and friends and family members are mourning over you, what would you like to hear them say about you?"

The first guy immediately responds, "I would like to hear them say that I was one of the great doctors of my time, and a great family man."

The second guy says, "I would like to hear that I was a wonderful husband and school teacher who made a huge difference in the children of tomorrow."

The last guy thinks a minute and replies, "I guess I'd like to hear them say, 'Look, he's moving!"

## Definitions

College :- A place where some pursue learning and others learn pursuing.

Etc :- A sign to make others believe that you know more than you actually do.

Office :- A place where you can relax after your strenuous life at home.

Ecstasy :- A feeling when you feel you are going to feel a feeling you have never felt before.

Committee :- Individuals who can do nothing individually and sit to decide that nothing can be done together.

Politician :- One who shakes your hand before elections and our confidence after.

Smile :- A curve that can set a lot of things straight.

Optimist :- A person who starts taking bath if he accidently falls into a river.

Pessimist :- A person who says that O is the last letter in ZERO, instead of the first letter in word OPPORTUNITY.

Diplomat :- A person who tells you to go to hell in such a way that you actually look forward to the trip.

Classic :- A book which people praise, but do not read.

Divorce :- Future tense of marriage.

Father :- A banker provided by nature.

Rumor :- News that travels at the speed of sound.

Criminal :- A guy no different from the rest of us...except that he got caught.

Worry :- Interest paid on trouble before it falls due.

Boss :- Someone who is early when you are late and late when you are early.

Philosopher :- A fool who torments himself during life, to be spoken of when dead.

Tears :- The hydraulic force by which masculine power is defeated by feminine power.

Yawn :- The only time some married men ever get to open their mouth.

Experience :- The name men give to their mistakes.

Atom Bomb: - An invention to end all inventions.

Doctor :- A person who kills your ills by pills, and then kills you with his bills.

Engineer :- One who is paid for sending and receiving such junk mails

## One Dark Holi Night

Two men were walking home after a Holi party and decided to take a shortcut through the cemetery just for laughs. Right in the middle of the cemetery they were startled by a tap-tap-tapping noise coming from the misty shadows. Trembling with fear, they found an old man with a hammer and chisel, chipping away at one of the headstones.

"Holy cow, Mister," one of them said after catching his breath, "You scared us to death-we thought you were a ghost! What are you doing working here so late at night?"

"Those fools!" the old man grumbled. "They misspelled my name!"

## Squeezing a lemon

A bartender in a Bangalore bar squeezed a lemon completely and offered his patrons one thousand rupees to anyone who can further squeeze a drop out of the lemon. One guy weighing about 120 kilos tried hard to squeeze the lemon but nothing came out. The bartender asked him what he did for living? The patron told him he was a wrestler.

Then a tall guy came and tried and he could also not squeeze the lemon. He was a cricketer. Slowly everyone in the bar tried in vain. At the end of the day, a small and thin guy came and he squeezed three drops of juice from the lemon. Everyone in the bar was pleasantly surprised. The bartender asked the man what he did for living? The man replied he was an Income Tax Officer with the Government of India.

## Full name

Mr. Ramchandani moved from Kutub Nagar to Ahmedabad. He worked hard, saved every rupee he earned and started a small business. Slowly he started making lots of money and one day he wanted to deposit the money in a bank. He was illiterate and when he opened his account he wrote XX at the place where a signature was needed. Mr. Ramchandani prospered, opened lots of stores and bought a fancy house.

One day his banker came to his house with lots of checks. Mr. Ramchandani used to sign his checks with two X's

However, more recently, he has been signing the checks with three X's. The banker wanted to check that as Mr. Ramchandani's signature on the record was only two X's Mr. Ramchandani looked embarrassed and said, "I am sorry about making trouble. You see my wife said that since I am now in such a high class rich society, I should have a middle name."

## Giving a gift

A man was looking for a gift for a friend. Everything was too expensive except for a glass vase that had been broken, which he could purchase for only one rupee. He asked the store to send it, hoping his friend would think it has been broken in transit.

In due time, he received an acknowledgment. "Thanks for the vase," it read.

"It was so thoughtful of you to wrap each piece separately."

## Magnitude of things

A man was asleep and God came to him in a dream. God said, "Is there anything you'd like to ask me?"

The man thought for a minute and then he said, "Yes. What is a crore rupees to you?"

God said, "Well, a crore rupees are like a paisa to me."

The man asked, "What is a hundred years like to you?"

God said, "A hundred years is like a second to me."

The man said, "God can I borrow a paisa from you?"

God said, Sure. "Just a second."

## Two farmers

In a village Anjanbihari in Madhya Pradesh, two farmers were bragging about the size of their farms.

First farmer said, "I recently bought a farm that is about one thousand-acre big."

Second farmer said, "Let me put this way, My farm is so big that when I drive through it in my tractor at sunrise, I keep going and going and at even at the sunset, I cannot see the other end of the farm."

The first farmer said, "Oh! - Even I used to have a tractor like that!"

## A guardian angel

A man was walking in the street when she heard a voice.

"Stop! Stand still! If you take one more step, a brick will fall down on your head and kill you."

The woman stopped and a big brick fell right in front of her. The woman was astonished. She went on, and after awhile she was going to cross the road. Once again the voice shouted:

"Stop! Stand still! If you take one more step a car will run over you, and you will die."

The woman did as she was instructed, just as a car came careening around the corner, barely missing her.

"Where are you?" the woman asked. "Who are you?"

"I am your guardian angel," the voice answered.

"Oh, yeah?" the woman asked. "And where the hell were you when I got married?"

## Directions please

A city couple were driving in the country and stopped in a one horse town to ask a local how to get back on the highway.

He scratched his head and said. "I don't think you can get there from here."

"It's no use asking him," said the woman to her husband, "He's stupid"

"Me? Stupid?" exclaimed the local. "I'm not the one's that's lost. You are!"

## A bald man

A bald man took a seat in a beauty shop.

"How can I help you?" asked the stylist.

"I went for a hair transplant," the guy explained, "but I couldn't stand the pain. If you can make my hair look like yours without causing me any discomfort, I'll pay you Rs.5000."

"No problem," said the stylist, and she quickly shaved her head.

"[illegible]," the woman asked. "Who are you?"

"I am your guardian angel," the voice answered.

"Oh yeah?" the woman asked. "And where the hell were you when I got married?"

## Directions please

A city couple were driving in the country and stopped in a one-horse town to ask a local how to get back on the highway.

He scratched his head and said, "I don't think you can get there from here."

"It's no use asking him," said the woman to her husband. "He's stupid."

"Me? Stupid?" exclaimed the local. "I'm not the one that's lost. You are!"

## A bald man

A bald man walked into a beauty shop.

"How can I help you?" asked the stylist.

"I went for a hair transplant," the guy explained, "but I couldn't stand the pain. If you can make my hair look like yours without causing me any discomfort, I'll pay you [illegible]."

"No problem," said the stylist, and she quickly shaved her head.

# Morons

## A Trip to Mumbai

A flight attendant encountered a moron sitting in the first class section with a business class ticket at New Delhi Airport. She told her she would not be able to sit in that section but the moron refused to move. She said, "I'm a moron, I'm beautiful, I'm going to Mumbai and you can't make me move."

The flight attendant went to the head attendant who went to the lady and again asked her to move because she was sitting in the first class section and didn't belong there.

Again the lady said, "I'm a moron, I'm beautiful, I'm going to Mumbai, and you can't make me move."

Finally, in exasperation the flight attendants went to the pilot and explained the situation.

He replied, "Oh, I can take care of that. My wife is a moron."

He went back and whispered something to the lady, and she immediately got up and walked back to the business section.

The others were curious as to why she responded so fast to him and asked for an explanation.

The pilot said, "Oh, it was simple. I just told her that the first class section wasn't going to Mumbai."

## First time on a Boeing

A moron gets an opportunity to fly to a nearby country. He has never been on an airplane anywhere and was very excited and tense.

As soon as he boarded the plane, a Boeing747, he started jumping in excitement, running over seat to seat and started shouting,

"BOEING 747! BOEING 747!! BOEING 747!!! BO...."

He, sort of, forgets where he is, even the pilot in the cockpit hears the noise. Annoyed by the goings on, the Pilot comes out and shouts, "BE SILENT!"

There was pin-drop silence everywhere, and everybody is looking at the moron and the angry Pilot. He stared at the pilot in silence for a moment and then, all of a sudden, started shouting,"OEING 747! OEING 747!! OEING 747!!! O

## Driving Moron

There was this Moron driving up to a red light at a busy intersection. For some reason, his car just stopped running. The light changed from green to red, and the man behind his got impatient. The light changed green and he still didn't move.

By now, the man was exasperated and began honking his horn in frustration.

Two more light changes took place, and the Moron still didn't move. So, he kept up his incessant honking....

The Moron got out of his car and went to the man who was behind him.

He asked him to roll his window down.

The man rudely demanded, "What is the matter?"

To which the Moron replied, "Well, if you will come up there and start my car, I will come back here and honk your horn for you."

## TGIF

A business man got on an elevator in a building. When he entered the elevator, there was a moron lady already inside and she greeted him by saying "T-G-I-F".

He smiled at her and replied "S-H-I-T".

She looked at him, puzzled, and said "T-G-I-F" again.

He acknowledged her remark again by answering "S-H-I-T."

The moron was trying to be friendly, so she smiled her biggest smile and said as sweetly as possibly, "T-G-I-F" another time.

The man smiled back to her and once again replied with a quizzical expression,

"S-H-I-T".

The moron finally decided to explain things, and this time she said, "T-G-I-F, T-hank G-oodness I-ts F-riday; get it?" The man answered, "S-orry H-oney, I-t's T-hursday".

## An interview

The executive was interviewing a young Moron for a position in his company. He wanted to find out something about his personality so he asked, "If you could have a conversation with someone, living or dead, who would it, be?"

The Moron quickly responded, "The living one."

## A diver

A diver has been enjoying an aquatic world near Kanyakumari, twenty feet below the sea level. He saw another guy swimming at the same depth but without any Scuba gear. He went down thirty and then forty feet depth and the other guy was there without any Scuba gear! The diver wrote on a waterproof chalkboard how in the world the other guy was able to stay under this deep without Scuba gear? The other guy wrote back on the chalkboard, "I am drowning, you moron, please help"

## Capital of Bihar

A moron was bragging about her knowledge of the state capitals in India. She proudly said," go ahead, ask me, I know all of them."

Her friend said, "O.K., what's the capital of Bihar?"

The moron replied, "Oh, that's easy, "B".

## Helicopter

How did the moron explain how his helicopter crashed?

He said it was getting cold, so he turned off the ceiling fan.

## Hotdog

Two morons from a small town were visiting Goa for the first time when they saw a hot dog vendor. Not having street vendors back home they decided to have this new experience.

After getting their orders the first moron turned to the second and said "What part of the dog did you get?"

[illegible] said, "Oh, what's the meaning of that?"

The foreign replied [illegible] "I [illegible]"

**Helicopter**

[illegible] the [illegible] pilot [illegible] helicopter [illegible]

[illegible] it was [illegible] [illegible] heading [illegible]

**Protection**

Two hunters from a [illegible] were getting [illegible] for the first time [illegible] not dog [illegible] back home they decided to give this new experience.

After getting their [illegible] the first hunter turned to the second and said "What part of the dog did you get?"

# Office

## An interview

During a job interview an employer asked a fresh Delhi IIT graduate

What starting salary are you looking for?"

About 125,000 Rupees per month depending upon the benefits, four weeks of vacation and a signing bonus, the graduate said.

The employer said 'I could give you a salary of 200,000 Rupees per month, six weeks of vacation and a red Maruti as a signing bonus."

Are you kidding Sir, asked the IIT graduate?

Employer said, " yes, but you started it."

## Life after death

One day an employer asked a new employee

"Do you believe in life after death?"

Yes Sir, the employee said.

Well, that makes every thing fine, said the employer.

The employee asked his boss why he asked him that question.

The employer replied": After you left early yesterday to attend the funeral for your grandmother, she stopped by in the office to see you."

## Rest in peace

Once two things happened on the same day. Tatas opened a factory in Faridabad and on the same day a branch manager working for Tatas in Moradabad lost his mother. The boss of Tatas asked his secretary to send flowers and a personal note for both occasions.

The branch manager at his new branch in Faridabad got a message saying "Rest in peace." When the boss came to know this, he was angry and called his secretary and told her about the mistake. The secretary said that "I am really sorry for the mistake but rather than getting angry at me you should imagine this. The mother of the branch manager in Moradabad who was being buried on that day, received a note from me saying, Congratulations on your new location."

## Forgot my watch

An industrialist is giving a speech at his share holders meeting about the progress made by their company. He gets a bit carried away and talks for two hours instead of scheduled 15 minutes. Finally, he realizes what he has done and says; "I'm sorry I talked so long. I left my watch at home."

A voice from the back of the room says, "But, there's a calendar behind you."

## Two Words

The other day I had the opportunity to drop by my department head's office. He is a friendly guy and on the rare opportunities that I have to pay him a visit, we have had enjoyable conversations. While I was in his office yesterday I asked him, "Sir, what is the secret of your success?"

He said, "Two words." And, Sir, what are they?"

"Right decisions." "But how do you make right decisions?"

"One word." he responded. "And, sir, what is that?"

"Experience." "And how do you get experience?"

"Two words." And, Sir, what are they?"

"Wrong decisions."

## TEN BEST THINGS TO SAY IF YOU GET CAUGHT SLEEPING AT YOUR DESK

#10. "They told me at the blood bank this might happen."

#9. "This is just a 15-minute power nap like they raved about in that time-management course you sent me to."

#8. "Whew! Guess I was just concentrating on the next task. You probably got here just in time"

#7. "I wasn't sleeping. I was meditating on the mission statement and envisioning a new paradigm."

#6. "I was testing my keyboard for drool resistance."

#5. "I was doing a highly specific yoga exercise to relieve work-related stress. Are you discriminating against people who practice yoga?"

#4. "Why did you interrupt me? I had almost figured out a solution to our company's biggest problem."

#3. "The coffee machine is broken...."

#2. "Someone must have put decaffeinated coffee in the wrong pot...."And the #1 best thing to say if you get caught sleeping at your desk:

#1. "... And, finally, let us pray for the future of our company. Amen."

## Differences Between You and Your Boss

When you take a long time, youre slow.

When your boss takes a long time, he's thorough.

When you don't do it, you're lazy.

When your boss doesn't do it, he's too busy.

When you make a mistake, you're an idiot.

When your boss makes a mistake, he's only human.

When doing something without being told, you're overstepping your authority.

When your boss does the same thing, that's initiative.

When you take a stand, you're being bull-headed.

When your boss does it, he's being firm.

When you overlooked a rule of etiquette, you're being rude.

When your boss skips a few rules, he's being original.

When you please your boss, you're chamcha.

When your boss pleases his boss, he's being cooperative.

When you're out of the office, you're wandering around.

When your boss is out of the office, he's on business.

When you're on a day off sick, you're always sick.

When your boss is a day off sick, he must be very ill.

When you apply for leave, you must be going for an interview.

When your boss applies for leave, it's because he's overworked.

## Sweeping the floor

A college graduate applied for a job in a departmental store in Mumbai. On the first day of the job the owner of the store gave him a broom and told him that his first task was to sweep the floor.

The graduate was taken aback and told the employer, "Sir, but I am a college graduate."

The employer said, "Oh....I did not know that. Here, give me the broom and I will show you how to do it."

## Looking for a job

Kundan and Rupo went to a big city to get jobs. They saw a "Now Hiring" sign at a place that turned out to be a bar. The receptionist told them that the owner of the bar was conducting the interview in his office inside the bar. Kundan went first for the interview.

The owner of the bar was a stout man, lots of scars on his face from the old wounds and instead of ears he had two tiny holes in the sides of his head. The man told that working in the bar was tough and required lots of perception. The interview was about how good a candidate was at noticing the things. He asked Kundan to look around the room and tell him what he noticed. Kundan looked around and said, "I see lots of liquor bottles, polished glasses, chrome plated furniture." He then looked at the owner and told him, "I also notice that you have no ears!" Hearing that the owner got angry, he jumped out his chair, grabbed Kundan from the neck and threw him out of the office."

It was now Rupo's turn to go for the interview. Kundan told Rupo, "Whatever you do inside - don't talk about his ears as he gets wild." Rupo said that he will remember that and went inside to face the owner.

The owner repeated that working in the bar was tough and required lots of perception. The interview was about how perceptive a candidate was. He asked Rupo to look around the room and tell him what he noticed. Rupo looked around and said, "I see lots of liquor bottles, polished glasses, chrome plated furniture." He then looked at the owner and said, "And you wear contact lenses."

The owner stood up in the amazement. "That is awesome perception! How could you tell that from way over there?"

Rupo replied, "It is obvious. You cannot wear glasses as you have no ears!"

# Police

## He has been drinking

To celebrate their honeymoon one couple drove from New Delhi to Simla. The husband was driving the car on the highway when a highway patrolman pulled their car. The cop told the husband that he was doing 80 miles in a 55-mile zone.

I was only going 55, said the husband

Not according to my radar, the cop said

Yes, I was, the guy shouted back.

No, you were not the cop said With that wife of the man leaned toward the window and said,

"Officer, I should warn you not to argue with my husband when he has been drinking."

## Pullover

One day a lady was driving her Maruti on a highway and while driving she started knitting. A highway patrolman came alongside her speeding car and was astounded to see that behind the wheels, the lady was knitting. The cop cranked down his window and yelled Pullover.

No, the lady yelled back, it is a scarf.

## Shut up

A family had three sons. The eldest son was very talkative. Ever since he was three years old, he could talk continuously. One day his mother got fed up so much that she named him Shut up. On the other hand middle son was loud and noisy. His mother used to call him Be quiet. The youngest son turned out to be very mischievous and his mother named him the Trouble. One day all three kids, Shut up, Be quiet and Trouble were being very rowdy at home so their mother threw them out of the house-that used to be her favorite way of punishing them.

While playing out in the woods, Trouble disappeared. Both elder brothers- Shut up and Be quiet were looking for their little brother. They met a cop and asked him to find their little brother. The cop told them to calm down and give him basic information.

What is your name son he asked the oldest brother.

"Shut up," he said excitedly.

Don" be smart with me boy, said the cop.

Now let us see whether your brother can answer a simple question. What is your name?

"Be quiet" said the second brother. The cop was upset by

now and said

"Are you looking for trouble?"

Yes, where is he? Asked the boys.

## Long wait

Did you hear about the kid who was pulled over for speeding?

The cop got out of his car and the young man rolled down his window.

"I've been waiting for you all day," the cop said.

The guy replied, "Yeah, well I got here as fast as I could."

When the cop finally stopped laughing, he sent the kid on his way without a ticket.

## You are on radar

An off-duty police officer, familiar with radar guns, drove through a school

zone within the legal speed limit when the flash of a camera went off, taking a picture of his license plate. The officer, thinking the radar was in error, drove by again; even more slowly. Another flash. He did it again for a third time, at an even slower speed. Same result. "This guy must have screwed up the settings," the off-duty officer thought. A few weeks later, when he received the violations in the mail, he discovered three traffic tickets: each for not wearing a seat belt!

## Law & Order

A policeman stops a lady in New Delhi and asks for her license. He says, "Lady, it says here that you should be wearing glasses."

The woman answered, "Well, I have contacts."

The policeman replied, "I don't care who you know! You're getting a ticket!"

## Drinking

Late one Friday night the policeman spotted a man driving very erratically through the streets of Hyderabad. They pulled the man over and asked him if he had been drinking that evening.

"Aye, so I have. 'This Friday, you know, so me and the lads stopped by the pub where I had six or seven pints. And then there was something called "Happy Hour" and they served these mar-gar-itos which are quite good. I had four or five o' those. Then I had to drive my friend Mike home and O' course I had to go in for a couple of Guinness - Couldn't be rude, ye know. Then I stopped on the way home to get another bottle for later." And the man fumbled around in his coat until he located his bottle of whiskey, which he held up for inspection. The officer sighed,

and said, "Sir, I'm afraid I'll need you to step out of the car and take a breath analyzer test."

Indignantly, the man said, "Why? Don't ye believe me?!"

## Effect of Diagrams

Two young guys were picked up by the cops for smoking dope and appeared in court on Friday before the judge. The judge said, "You seem like nice young men, and I'd like to give you a second chance rather than jail time. I want you to go out this weekend and try to show others the evils of drug use and get them to give up drugs forever. I'll see you back in court Monday."

Monday, the two guys were in court, and the judge said to the 1st one, "How did you do over the weekend?"

"Well, your honor, I persuaded 17 people to give up drugs forever."

"17 people? That's wonderful. What did you tell them?"

"I used a diagram, your honor. I drew two circles, onesmall and one large.

and told them the big circle is your brain before drugs and the small circle is your brain after drugs."

"That's admirable," said the judge.

"And you, how did you do?"(to the 2nd boy)

"Well, your honor, I persuaded 156 people to give up drugs forever."

"156 people! That's amazing! How did you manage to do that?!"

"Well, I used a similar approach, drew two circles, one small and one large.

I said, (pointing to the small circle) "This is your butt hole before prison..."

and (pointing to the large circle) 'This is your butt hole when you leave prison".

## Mistaken Drunk

A drunk phoned police to report that thieves had been in his car. "They've stolen the dashboard, the steering wheel, the brake pedal, even the accelerator," he cried out.

However, before the police investigation could start, the phone rang a second time, and the same voice came over the line, "Never mind," he said with a hiccup, "I got in the back seat by mistake!"

## Excuses for driving accidents

What follows are REAL excuses from drivers when asked to sum up their accident in the fewest words possible:

1. The pedestrian had no idea which way to run, so I ran over him.

2. I thought my window was down, but I found it was up when I put my head through it.

3. The guy was all over the road, I had to swerve a number of times before I hit him.

4. The other car collided with mine without giving warning of its intention.

5. I collided with a stationary truck which was coming the other way.

6. A truck backed through my windshield into my wife's face.

7. My car was legally parked as it backed into the other vehicle.

8. I was sure the old fellow would never make it to the other side of the road when I struck him.

9. A pedestrian hit me and went under my car.

10. In an attempt to kill a fly, I drove into a telephone pole.

## Frequent visitor

The Judge said to the defendant, "I thought I told you I never wanted to see you in here again."

"Your Honor," the criminal said, "that's what I tried to tell the police, but they wouldn't listen."

## Speeding lady

One day a certain lady is driving on the Highway... and she frequently checks her speed gauge to make sure she stays within the speed limit. But when she looks into her rear mirror, much to her dismay, she sees a police car not far behind! And to make matters worse, the police car turned on the siren & flashing lights. She thought to herself, "Uh-oh, what have I done now? I'm not speeding. I'm not drinking. I have my seat belt on! I have kept up my license dues and everything!"

Presently, she pulls over and the police car pulls over to the side right behind her car. She drove her car slowly to a stop, slowly rolled down the window, and prepared for a ticket when she knew she didn't deserve it. A policeman walked up to her window, and spoke to her. The lady pointed to her ear and shook her head, meaning she was deaf. The policeman smiled slightly, saying, "I know. I'm here to tell you that your horn is stuck!"

# Politics

## Keeping One's Composure

A well-known Indian politician was one day invited to a university to give a lecture to the students. Before he could begin speaking to the large group assembled in the auditorium, a very unkempt looking student at the back shouted a vulgar word at him. The word ringed in everyone's ears. There was a shocked silence but the politician, keeping his composure, said: "Now that you've given us your name, what's your question?"

## Where is the brain?

A politician, who was very small-sized, was often derided by an opponent, a tall, well-built man. One day the opponent walked up to him, looked down sneeringly and said loudly: "You know, I could just swallow you up!"

"In that event," said the little fellow, looking up," you would have more brains in your stomach than you'll ever have in your head!"

## Which end of fork?

At a dinner party for politicians, one of the guests, an obnoxiously loud young man, tried to make clever remarks about everyone and everything. He was served a piece of meat, he picked it up with his fork, held it up and smirked: "Is this pig?"

Another guest, sitting opposite, asked quietly:

"Which end of the fork are you referring to?"

## American space program

In the early days of the American space program, NASA received reports from the astronauts that their pens would not write in the space. Ball points, fountain pens, even quills, nothing worked! So NASA contacted the people who had supplied the pens and made money available for the production of a pen which would write in the space. Eventually, thousands of dollars later, a suitable pen was produced, incorporating a small gas filled cylinder which propelled the ink out of the pen. It worked both in the space and underwater. The problem was solved, albeit at great expense. Many years later, when cooperation with the Russians was established, it occurred to someone at NASA to ask how the Russians had solved the problem. There was no problem, they said, we used a pencil!!

## Exchanging Generals

Recently, following the Kargil conflict with the Pakistan, Prime Minister Atal Behari Vajpayee visited the United States and met with President Bill Clinton. In order to promote military collaboration between India and US, President Clinton suggested to Mr. Vajpayee that there should be exchange of two Generals between the US and India. Mr. Vajpayee heard President Clinton's proposal patiently and replied, "India will give General Manekshah and General Kareeapa to the US and America should give General Electric and General Motors to India."

## A Lesson in Political Science

Socialism:

You have two cows. The government takes one to give to someone else.

Communism:

You have two cows. The government takes both and gives you the milk.

Fascism:

You have two cows. The government takes both and sells you the milk.

Nazism:

You have two cows. The government takes both and shoots you.

Bureaucracy:

You have two cows. The government takes both, shoots one and pours the milk down the drain.

Capitalism:

You have two cows. You sell one and buy a bull.

Anarchy:

You steal neighbors bull, and shoot the government.

## Elections

Are there any historical precedents for the elections in Pakistan?

Yes, in the story of the creation. God made Eve, put her in the Garden of Eden, and said to Adam:

"Now choose a woman."

## Election in China

In Beijing, a dejected Communist Party candidate trudges home after the polls close.

"So, Lin, how many votes did you get?" asks his wife.

"Two,""he responds.

She slaps him hard across the face.

"What was that for?"

"For having a mistress!"

## The environment

In an underdeveloped country, don't drink the water.

In a developed country, don't breath the air.

# Religion

## Jewish Sons

A Jewish father was concerned about his son who was sorely lacking in his knowledge of the Jewish faith. To remedy this he sent his son to Israel to experience his heritage. A year later the young man returned home

"Father, thank you for sending me to the and of our Fathers,"the son said. "It was wonderful and enlightening, however, I must confess that while in Israel I converted to Christianity."

"Oy vey," replied the father, "what have I done." So in the tradition of the patriarchs, he went to his best friend and sought his advice and solace.

"It is amazing that you should come to me," stated his friend, "I too sent my son to Israel and he returned a Christian."

So in the tradition of the patriarchs, they went to the Rabbi. "It is amazing that you should come to me," stated the Rabbi, "I too sent my son to Israel and he returned a Christian. What is happening to our sons?"

Brothers, we must take this to the Lord," said the Rabbi. They fell to their knees and began to wail and pour out their hearts to the Almighty".

As they prayed the clouds above opened and a Mighty Voice stated,

"Amazing that you should come to me."

I, too, sent My Son to Israel . . . and he became Christian.

## Service

One Sunday morning, the pastor in Nagaland noticed little Alex was staring up at the large plaque that hung in the foyer of the church. It was covered with names, and small Indian flags were mounted on either side of it.

The seven-year-old had been staring at the plaque for some time, so the pastor walked up, stood beside the boy, and said quietly, "Good morning Alex." "Good morning pastor," replied the young man, still focused on the plaque.

"Pastor, what is this?" Alex asked. "Well, son, it's a memorial to all the young men and women who died in the service."

Soberly, they stood together, staring at the large plaque. Little Alex's voice was barely audible when he asked, "Which service, the 9:00 or the 10:30?"

## Church service

A Sunday school teacher asked her little children, as they were on the way to church service, "And why is it necessary to be quiet in church?"

One bright little girl replied, "Because people are sleeping."

## Insured voice

A Gyani, the man who sings the prayers at a Gurdwara, brags before his congregation in a booming, bellowing voice: "Two years ago I insured my voice with Lloyds of London for Rs.750,000."

There is a hushed and awed silence in the crowded room. Suddenly, from the back of the room, the quiet, nasal voice of an elderly woman is heard, "So what did you do with the money?"

## Creating a human being

One day a group of scientists got together and decided that man had come a long way and no longer needed God. So they picked one scientist to go and tell God that they were done with him.

The scientist walked up to God and said, "God, we've decided that we no longer need you. We're to the point that we can clone people and do many miraculous things, so why don't you just go on and get lost."

God listened very patiently and kindly to the man and after the scientist was done talking, God said, "Very well, how about this, let's say we have a man making contest."

To which the scientist replied, "OK, great!"

But God added, "Now, we're going to do this just like I did back in the old days to create Adam."

The scientist said, "Sure, no problem" and bent down and grabbed himself a handful of dirt to create a man.

God just looked at him and said, "No, no, no. You go get your own dirt!"

## Modern Technology

Nine-year-old Joey was asked by his mother what he had learned in Sunday School. "Well, Mom, our teacher told us how God sent Moses behind enemy lines on a rescue mission to lead the Israelites out of Egypt. When he got to the Red Sea, he had his engineers build a pontoon bridge, and all the people walked across safely. He used his walkie-talkie to radio headquarters and call in an air strike."

They sent in bombers to blow up the bridge and all the Israelites were saved.

"Now, Joey, is that REALLY what your teacher taught you?" his mother asked.

"Well, no, Mom, but if I told it the way the teacher did, you would never believe it!"

## Baptism

A father is in church with three of his young children, including his five-year-old daughter. As was customary, he sat in the very front row so that the children could properly witness the service. During this particular service, the minister was performing the baptism of a tiny infant. The little five-year-old girl was taken by this, observing that he was saying something and pouring water over the infant's head. With a quizzical look on her face, the little girl turned to her father and asked: "Daddy, why is he brainwashing that baby??"

## Quick Swim

A minister, a priest and a rabbi went for a hike one day. It was very hot.They were sweating and exhausted when they came upon a small lake. Since it was fairly secluded, they took off all their clothes and jumped in the water. Feeling refreshed, the trio decided to pick a few berries while enjoying their "freedom." As they were crossing an open area, who should come along but a group of ladies from town. Unable to get to their clothes in time, the minister and the priest covered their privates, and the rabbi covered his face while they ran for cover.

After the ladies had left, and the men got their clothes back on, the minister and the priest asked the rabbi why he covered his face rather than his privates. The rabbi replied,"I don't know about you, but in MY congregation, it's my face they would recognize."

## Smooth Delivery

A preacher, who shall we say was "humor impaired," attended a conference to help encourage and better prepare pastors for their ministry. Among the speakers were many well known and dynamic speakers. One such speaker boldly approached the pulpit and, gathering the entire crowd's attention, said, "The best years of my life were spent in the arms of a woman that wasn't my wife!" The crowd was shocked! He followed up by saying, "And that woman was my mother!"- The crowd burst into laughter and the speaker delivered the rest of his talk, which went over quite well.

The next week, the pastor decided he'd give this humor thing a try, and use that joke in his sermon. As he surely approached the pulpit that sunny Sunday, he tried to rehearse the joke in his head. It suddenly seemed a bit foggy to him. Getting to the microphone he said loudly, "The greatest years of my life were spent in the arms of another woman that was not my wife!" The congregation inhaled half the air in the room. After standing there for almost 10 seconds in the stunned silence, trying to recall the second half of the joke, the pastor finally blurted out, "...and I can't remember who she was!"

## Wrong address

One beggar was begging in a temple near Connaught place. Many devotees came by and gave him five or 10 paisa. Some of the devotees gave him nothing. A guy was coming back from a nearby bar and saw that the beggar was not getting much money. He gave the beggar a five-rupee note and told the beggar to beg near the bar instead of temple. The beggar went near the bar and started begging. Very soon he accumulated lot of money as patrons coming out of the bar were giving him notes of 5, 10 and in some cases 20 rupees. At the end of the day, the beggar looked towards the sky and said to the almighty "You are something else, you gaveme temple as your residential address but you live somewhere else!"

## Haldiram ki Bhujia

In November 1999 Pope Paul visited New Delhi and met with Mr. Haldiram. Catholic prayer before eating says, "Thank you lord for giving us this bread."

Mr. Haldiram offered one crore rupees to the church if the Pope recommends replacing the word "bread" with the "Haldiram ki Bhujia" in the Catholic prayer. Pope told Mr. Haldiram that he would discuss the proposal with his cardinals in the Vatican. When the Pope returned to Rome and met with the cardinals, he told them about the proposal and said that there was a good and bad news about the proposal. The good news was that the church was going to get Rs. one crore from Mr. Haldiram. What was the bad news about the proposal, anxious cardinals asked? The pope replied, "The bad news is that we will loose our donation of Rs, 20 lakhs from the Modern Bread Bakery."

## Two notes

Two notes, a one-rupee note and other a twenty-rupee note were good friends. They used to be together for a long time. Unfortunately, they got separated for a year.

One day by chance they met and were excited to see each other. One-rupee note asked the twenty-rupee note where he had been for such a long time. Twenty-rupee note replied jubilantly that he had a wonderful time in watching a soccer game played by Mohan Bagan and East Bengal, enjoying a concert by Lata Mangeshkar, and finally traveling all over India by Indian airlines. Twenty-rupee note then asked where the

one-rupee note had been for such a long time. The one-rupee note replied sheepishly,
"What to tell you dear friend, it is always mandir or gurdwara, mandir or gurdwara......"

## Facelift

A wealthy middle-aged lady was rushed to a hospital following a heart attack. She was a religious person and saw God in a dream like state. She asked God whether that was the end of her? God told her that he was very happy with her devotion and told her that not only she would recover from the heart attack but was also going to live for another forty years. The lady thanked God, and recovered completely. She thought since she was going to live for quite a while, she must go through surgical procedures to make her look good while she was in the hospital. She went through facelifting, breast augmentation and liposuction to reduce her weight. She looked wonderful and was released from the hospital after a month.

When she was just coming out of the hospital, she was run over by an ambulance and died. She went to the heaven and met God there. She complained to God that she was told by him that she was going to live for another forty years and here she died so soon. God replied, "Lady, while in the hospital you changed so much that even I could not recognize you."

## Doing well in maths

Little Satu was not doing well in his math class. His parents tried tutors, flash cards, learning centers but nothing worked. His parents then enroled him in a catholic school. On the very first day, Satu came home and instead of playing outside, kept working on his math homework. Within a couple of weeks he was doing very well in his math class. Satu's parents were surprised at his tremendous efforts to well in maths. They were curious to know what turned him around, "Was it the nuns, or the books, or the discipline in the school? Little Satu looked at his parents and said, "Well, on the first day of school, when I saw that guy nailed to the plus sign, I knew they weren't fooling around!"

## Cab Driver

A Pujari and a Sardarji who used to drive a taxi in Old Delhi died and went to God. God was deciding who should go to first class heaven, second class heaven or hail. When Sardarji's turn came, God looked at his log book and told Sardarji to go to first class heaven. Sardarji thanked God and proceeded. Then the Pujari approached God, and again God looked at his log book, and told the Pujari to go to second class heaven."Just a minute," said the Pujari. "The Sardarji was a taxi-driver and he goes to first class heaven and I have been a Pujari for a long time and get to go to second class heaven. How can this be?"

"Up here, we go by results," said God. "While you preached, people used to sleep in the temple." "While Sardarji drove his taxi, people used to pray all the time."

## Going fishing

A young boy came to Sunday School late. His teacher knew that he was usually very prompt and asked him if anything was wrong.

The boy replied no, that he was going fishing but his dad told him that he needed to go to church. The teacher was very impressed and asked the boy if his dad had explained to him why it was more important to go to church than to go fishing. To which the boy replied, yes he did, dad said he didn't have enough bait for both of us.

## The preacher and old lady

What with sermon preparations and anxiety, the new preacher had gotten very little sleep the week before he was to address his flock for the first time; so by Sunday morning, he was both exhausted and extremely nervous. Nevertheless, he managed to make it up the few steps onto the platform and into the pulpit. However, he had barely begun his presentation when everything he had planned to say flew right out of his mind. In fact, his mind went totally blank. Then he remembered that in seminary they had taught him what to do if a situation like this ever arose:

"Repeat your last point, and let it remind you of what's coming next."

Figuring this advice couldn't hurt, he recalled the very last thing he'd said, and repeated it:

"Behold," he quoted, "I come quickly." Still his mind was

blank. He thought he'd better try it again: "Behold, I come quickly." Still nothing.

He tried it one more time-but in his panic, he pronounced the words with such force that he lost his balance, fell forward, knocked the pulpit to one side, tripped over a flower arrangement, and fell into the lap of a little old lady in the front row. Flustered and embarrassed, he picked himself up, apologized profusely, and started to explain what had just happened.

"That's all right, young man," said the little old lady kindly. "It was my fault, really. You told me three times you were on your way down here. I should have just gotten out of your way!"

## Dyslexic

Did you hear abut the dyslexic, agnostic, insomniac? He lays awake all night wondering if there really is a **dog**.

## Flood water

One day, the flood waters came to a small town in Madhya Pradesh on the Narmada River. The authorities came down the street in a small rowboat and found the local Pujari still standing on his front porch looking out over the water.

"Get in the boat, Pujari," they called out.

The Pujari answered, "No. I have faith in the Lord that he will take care of me." And the rowboat went away without him.

An hour later, the water had risen tremendously, and the next boatload of authorities found the Pujari on his balcony as the water kept climbing.

"Get in the boat, Pujari," they called out. "We're probably the last boat that'll come by."

The Pujari answered, "no. I have faith in the Lord that he will take care of me." And that rowboat, too, went away without him.

Another hour passed and the rising waters had forced the preacher onto his roof. A helicopter flew down toward him, and a loudspeaker boomed out, "Grab the rope, Pujari, and we'll pull you to safety! This is your last chance, but the water is rising fast!"

The Pujari answered, "No. I have faith in the Lord, that. He will take care of me." And the helicopter went away without him.

The flood waters finally engulfed the Pujari, and he found himself standing outside the gates of Heaven in front of very surprised God. God asked, "What are you doing here? It's not your time yet."

The Pujari answered, "I'm a little bit confused, myself. I had faith in you, and I thought you were going to take care of me."

God replied, "Well, we sent you two rowboats and a helicopter! What more did you want?"

# Romance

## Dear Diary

After dinner and a movie, a guy drove his date to a quiet country road and made his move. When the girl responded enthusiastically to his kissing, he tried sliding his hand up her blouse. Suddenly she jerked away, got out of the car and stomped home. That night, she wrote in her diary, "A girl's best friends are her own two legs." As long as two legs are together, I am fine.

On their next date, the guy returned to the country road. As they were necking, he slid his hand up girls' skirt. Once again, she pulled away, got out of the car and stomped home. That night, she wrote in her diary, "I repeat, a girl's best friends are her own two legs." As long as two legs are together, I am fine.

On the third date, the couple returned to the country road. This time, Mary did not get home until very late. That night she wrote, "Dear diary: There comes a time when even the best of friends must part."

## Sleeping Attire

The young bride's mother had some old-fashioned ideas of marriage, and passed them on to her daughter.

"Never let your husband see you in the nude," she advised. "You should always wear something."

"Yes, mother," replied the obedient girl.

Two weeks after the wedding, the girl and her brand-new husband were preparing to retire to bed when the guy asked,

"Dear, has there ever been any insanity in your family?"

"Not that I know of," she answered.

"Why?

"Well, we've been married for two weeks now and every night you've worn that silly hat to bed."

## Train to Chennai

The newlyweds were taking the train to Chennai. Cuddling together in an upper booth, they had a merry old time.

After the third marital joining, the bride said, "Darling, I just can't convince myself that we're really married."

From a berth halfway down the train, a deep voice bellowed, "Convince her!

I'd like to get some sleep!"

## Arriving Home

The newly married couple returned from their honeymoon. As they got off the plane at the crowded airport, the bride said,

"Darling, let's make the people think we've been married for a long time."

"Ok dear,:"said the husband. "Then you carry the bags."

## Speech Impediment

Over drinks one afternoon a buddy of mine and I were discussing former "loves." I told him that I once broke-up with a girl long ago because she had a seemingly incurable speech impediment.

Rahul said, "Suresh, I'm shocked. I never know you to be one to be prejudiced against handicaps. What was the girl's problem?"

Taking a sip, I paused and reflected. "She couldn't say 'Yes."

## Newly married on a train

The new husband had booked sleeping arrangements on the train, thinking he was going to have a roomette or compartment, only to find out he was on one side of the sleeping car in an upper bunk and his wife was in the other one across from him. About 12 o'clock he started feeling married so he said to his wife, "Hey honey, hey honey, why don't you come over here?"

His wife replied right back, "Well honey, how will I get over there?" to which he said, "Don't worry! I got something you can walk on." In answer to that, a fellow in the lower berth said, "Yeah, but how in Hell is she going to get back?"

## Stud Problems

An infamous stud with a long list of conquests walked into his neighborhood bar and ordered a drink. The bartender thought he looked worried and asked him if anything was wrong. "I'm scared out of my mind," the stud replied. "Some ticked-off husband wrote to me and said he'd kill me if I didn't stop messing with his wife."

"So stop," the barkeep said. I can't," the womanizer replied, taking a long swill. "The fellow didn't sign his name!"

## Sugar and Honey

A man goes to visit an old family friend, whom he hasn't seen in many years. All during the course of his visit, this friend refers to his wife in very affectionate terms, such as sugar, honey, cupcake, honey-buns, and biscuit.

The other man is quiet surprised at this, that after 70 years of marriage, his friend is still this taken with his "bride." He discretely asks of his friend, "how is it that after all this time, you are so much in love that you are able to refer to your wife in such loving terms?" To which the old man replies "To be quiet honest, I forgot her name over 10 years ago.

## Exhausted Newlyweds

The newlyweds were suffering from exhaustion. After an examination, their doctor advised, "It's not unusual for young people to overdo things during the first weeks of marriage. What you both need is rest. For the next month I want you to limit your sex life to those days of the week with an "r" in them. That is, Thursday, Friday and Saturday." Since the end of the week was approaching, the newlyweds had no immediate difficulty following the medico's orders. But on the first night of scheduled rest the young bride found herself eager as a beaver.. Hubby fell asleep, but she tossed and turned and finally nudged her spouse into partial wakefulness. Expecting daylight, and confused with the darkness, he asked, "What day is it honey?" She looked at him with a gleam in her eyes and says, "Mondray."

## This Bull Reproduced

A man takes his wife to the stock show. They start heading down the alley that had the bulls. They come up to the first bull and his sign stated: "This bull mated 50 times last year."

The wife turns to her husband and says, "He mated 50 times in a year, you could learn from him."

They proceed to the next bull and his sign stated: "This bull mated 65 times last year."

The wife turns to her husband and says, "This one mated 65 times last year. That is over five times a month. You can learn from this one, also."

They proceeded to the last bull and his sign said: "This bull mated 365 times last year."

The wife's mouth drops open and says, "WOW! He mated 365 times last year. That is ONCE A DAY!!! You could really learn from this one."

The man turns to his wife and says, "Go up and inquire if it was 365 times with the same cow."

## Wedding Bargains

A couple returned from their honeymoon and it's obvious to everyone that they are not talking to each other. The groom's best man takes him aside and asks what is wrong.

"Well," replied the man "when we had finished making love on the first night, as I got up to go to the bathroom, I put a 100-rupee note on the pillow without thinking."

"Oh, you shouldn't worry about that too much," said his friend. "I'm sure your wife appreciated that gesture.

The groom nodded gently and said, "I don't know if I can get over this, though. She gave me 30 rupee change!"

## The Cow

The only cow in a small town in Andhra Pradesh stopped giving milk. The people did some research and found that they could buy a cow from Punjab for 2,000 rupees, or one from Tamilnadu for 1,000 rupees. Being frugal, they bought the cow from Tamilnadu. The cow was wonderful. It produced lots of milk all the time, and the people were amazed and very happy. They decided to acquire a bull to mate with the cow and produce more cows like it. Then they would never have to worry about the milk supply again.

They bought a bull and put it in the pasture with their beloved cow. However, whenever the bull came close to the cow, the cow would move away. No matter what approach the bull tried, the cow would move away from the bull and he could not succeed in his quest.

The people were very upset and decided to ask a gyani, who was very wise, what to do. They told the gyani what was happening.

"Whenever the bull approaches our cow, she moves away. If he approaches from the back, she moves forward. When he approaches her from the front, she backs off. An approach from the side and she just walks away to the other side.

The gyani thought about this for a minute and asked, "Did you buy this cow from Tamilnadu?" The people were dumbfounded. They had never mentioned where they had gotten the cow. "You are truly a wise gyani. How did you know we got the cow from Tamilnadu?"

The gyani answered sadly, “My wife is from Tamilnadu."

# Shopping

## The Big Sale

It was the day of the big sale. Rumors of the sale (and some advertising in the local paper) were the main reason for the long line that formed by 8:30 a.m., the store's opening time, in front of the door. A small man pushed his way to the front of the line, only to be pushed back, amid loud and colorful curses. On the man's second attempt, he was punched square in the jaw, and knocked around a bit, and then thrown to the end of the line again. As he got up and tried the third time, he said to the person at the end of the line...

"That does it! If they hit me one more time, I won't open the store

## Waiter

A waiter brings the customer the stuffed nan he ordered with his thumb over the nan.

"Are you crazy?" yelled the customer, "with your hand on my nan?"

"What" answers the waiter, "You want me to drop it on the floor again?"

## Barber Surprised

There is this Good old Barber in Kansas City in the USA. One day a Florist goes to him for a haircut. After the cut, he goes to pay the Barber and the barber replies:

'I am Sorry, I cannot accept money from you; I am doing a Community Service'. The Florist is happy and leaves the shop.

The next morning when the Barber goes to open his shop, there is a Thank you Card and a dozen roses waiting at his door.

Next, a Cop goes for a haircut and he also goes to pay the Barber and the barber replies:

'I am Sorry, I cannot accept money from you; I am doing a Community Service'.

The Cop is happy and leaves the shop.

The next morning when the Barber goes to open his shop, there is a Thank you Card and a dozen Donuts waiting at his door.

Later, a Desi Software Engineer goes for a haircut and he also goes to pay the Barber and barber replies;

'I am Sorry, I cannot accept money from you; I am doing a Community Service'.

The next morning when the Barber goes to open his shop,

guess what he finds there -

A Dozen Desis waiting for a free Haircut......

## Vacuum Cleaner

This salesman selling vacuum cleaners is going from door to door trying to flog them to unsuspecting housewives. He goes to this new estate hoping to have some luck there. Carrying his cleaner up to the door and holding a bunch of goodies in his other hand, he knocks on the door.

"Excuse me madam," meanwhile pushing his way in the door. He quickly empties the goodies he has all over the lady's plush new wool carpet, including doggie stuff, gravel, dirt and an array of other stuff.

Then he pronounces: "The cleaners that I am about to sell you will clean all this or I vow that I will eat all the things I dropped on your carpet!"

The lady furious with the mess replies, "Well ,would you like sauce with that because we haven't got the power on yet!

## Instructions on the how to use goods

In case you needed further proof that the human race is doomed through stupidity, here are some actual label instructions on consumer goods:

On a hair dryer: Do not use while sleeping. (Gee, that's the only time I have to work on my hair!)

On a bag of potato chips: You could be a winner! No purchase necessary. Details inside. (The shoplifter special!)

On a bar of soap: Directions: Use like regular soap. (and that would be how)?

On some frozen dinners: Serving suggestion: Defrost. (But it's *just* a suggestion!)

On a dessert box: (Printed on bottom of the box) Do not turn upside down. (Too late! You lose!)

On a box of Bread Pudding: Product will be hot after heating. (Are you sure??? Let's experiment.)

On packaging for a steam iron: Do not iron clothes on body. (But wouldn't that save more time?)

On Children's cough medicine: Do not drive car or operate machinery. (We could do a lot to reduce the rate of construction accidents if we could just kept those five year olds off those fork lifts.)

On a sleep aid: Warning: may cause drowsiness. (One would hope!)

On a Korean kitchen knife: Warning keep out of children. (Or pets! What's for dinner?)

On a string of Chinese-made Christmas lights: For indoor or outdoor use only. (As opposed to use in outer space?)

On a Japanese food processor: Not to be used for the other use. (Now I'm curious.)

On a bag of peanuts: Warning: contains nuts. (Really?)

On an airline packet of nuts: Instructions: open packet, eat nuts. (I'm glad they cleared that up...)

On a child's superman costume: Wearing of this garment does not enable you to fly. (Sure, destroy a universal childhood fantasy!)

## Our friends

When we moved to Columbus, my son was three year old. Whenever we went for shopping we took our son with us and were delighted to talk to any person from India who happened to shop there. We used to recognize the fellow Indians by the way they dressed or looked. One day, while shopping in a grocery store I was concentrating on buying some vegetables and was not paying attention to other shoppers. Suddenly I heard my son screaming with joy "Daddy, Daddy, here are our friends", pointing towards some Indians shopping there.

## Indian dolls

One tourist was visiting Indian Dolls Museum in New Delhi. He saw many dolls on the display as well as other dolls that were on sale. He enquired the price of the dolls and was given the following price for various dolls.

The exercising doll: 100 rupees.

The bathing doll: 100 rupees.

The shopping doll: 100 rupees.

The dancing doll: 100 rupees.

The divorced doll: 20,000 rupees.

He was astonished to find that the divorced doll costed so

much and enquired why that doll was so expensive. He was told that the divorced doll came with her husband's house, scooter and furniture.

## Psychology

A very shy guy goes into a bar and sees a beautiful girl sitting at the bar.

After an hour of gathering up his courage he finally goes over to her and asks, "Would....you mind if I chatted with you for a while?"

The girl yelled at the top of her lungs, "No, I won't sleep with you tonight!"

Everyone in the bar was staring at them. The guy was completely embarrassed and he sat back at his table with his head down.

After a few minutes, the girl walked over to him and apologized. She smiled at him and said, "I am sorry if I embarrassed you. You see, I am a graduate student in psychology and I am doing research on how people respond to embarrassing situations."

To which he responded at the top of his lungs, "I cannot pay 2,000 rupees for a night!"

## Cheap perfume

After being away on business for a week before Christmas, Rajiv thought it would be nice to bring his wife a little gift.

"How about some perfume?" he asked the cosmetics clerk. She showed him a bottle costing Rs. 500.

"That's a bit much," said Rajiv, so she returned with a smaller bottle for Rs. 300.

"That's still quite a bit," Rajiv groused. Growing disgusted, the clerk brought out a tiny Rs.100 bottle.

Rajiv grew agitated. "What I mean," he said, "is I'd like to see something real cheap."

So the clerk handed him a mirror.

## Car Battery

An angry motorist went back to a garage where he'd purchased an expensive battery for his car six months earlier. "Listen," the motorist grumbled to the owner of the garage, "when I bought that battery you said it would be the last battery my car will ever need. It died after only six months!"

"Sorry," apologized the garage owner. "I didn't think your car would last longer than that."

## French fries

I stopped at a fast food restaurant recently. I was fascinated by a sign which offered fat free French fries. I decided to give them a try. I was dismayed when the clerk pulled a basket of fries from the fryer which were dripping with fat. He filled a bag with these fries and put them in my order.

"Just a minute!" I said. "Those aren't fat free."

"Yes, they are. We only charge for the potatoes.... The fat is free!"

## Chewy meat

Of the many kids in the junior high lunchroom, few had been brave enough to try the "mystery meat" but there was one boy who happened to have the stomach to try it. Disappointed, he picked up his tray and walked up to the cafeteria lady. "Ma'am, he said. "My meat is way too chewy." The lunch lady pulled out a fork and took a piece of the meat and put it in her mouth. "Chewy?" she exclaimed, "This has to be the most tender meat I've tasted!" The boy replied "Yes Ma'am, that's because that's the piece that I've been chewing on for the last half hour."

# Sports

## Golf club

After paying for his speeding ticket, a man was in a foul mood and stopped in a sporting good store to buy a golf club. He brought the club to the cash register.

Cash or charge? The clerk asked

Cash shouted the man. He realized his rudeness and explained to clerk how he paid for the speeding ticket and the judge made fun of him in the court.

Should I gift-wrap the club? The clerk asked or you are going back to the court to see the judge?

## Golf

One day a man was playing the game of golf when his Caddie Master walks over to him and says, "You're a foot past the tee-line. You'll have to move the ball back."The guy ignores him and continues to lineup her next shot. The Caddie Master repeats his instruction. Without taking his eyes off the ball, the guy said,

"Would someone please tell this clown that this is my second shot?"

## Cricket in heaven

Two buddies Sunil and Vijay were two of the biggest cricket fans in India. Their entire adult lives, Sunil and Vijay discussed cricket history in the winter, and they pored over every box score during the season. They went to many test matches a year. They even agreed that whoever died first would try to come back and tell the other if there was cricket in heaven.

One summer night, Sunil passed away in his sleep after watching India defeating Pakistan in New Delhi test match. He died happy.

A few nights later, his buddy Vijay awoke to the sound of Sunil's voice from beyond.

"Sunil," Is that you?" Vijay asked.

"Of course it me," Sunil replied.

"This is unbelievable!" Vijay exclaimed. "So tell me, is there cricket in heaven?"

"Well, I have some good news and some bad news for you. Which do you want to hear first?"

"Tell me the good news first," Vijay said

"Well, the good news is that yes there is cricket in heaven, said Sunil

"Oh, that is wonderful! So what could possibly be the bad news?", asked Vijay

"You're bowling tomorrow night," said Sunil.

## Cricket in Hell

St. Peter and Satan were having an argument one day about. Satan proposed a game to be played on neutral grounds between a select team from the heavenly host and his own hand-picked boys.

"Very well," said the gatekeeper of Heaven. "But you realize, I hope, that we've got all the good players and the best coaches."

"I know, and that's all right," Satan answered unperturbed, "We've got all the umpires."

## Psych Diagnosis

The psychology instructor had just finished a lecture on mental health and was giving an oral test. Speaking specifically about manic depression, she asked, "How would you diagnose a patient who walks back and forth screaming at the top of his lungs one minute, then sits in a chair weeping uncontrollably the next?"

A young man in the rear raised his hand and answered, "A basketball coach?"

## Boxing

Did you know that Mike Tyson has an upcoming bout with Prince Charles.

It seems that no one else has big enough ears to go 12 rounds.

# Travel

## Skydiving

A man goes for skydiving for the first time. After listening the instructions he is excited and jumps out of the airplane. After sometime, he pulls the ripcord. Nothing happens. He tries again. Still, nothing happens. He frantically begins to pull the cords of his back up parachute, but to no avail. Suddenly he looks down and he cannot believe his eyes. He sees a man coming up into air from the ground. Just as the other guy passes by, the skydiver-by this time scared out of his wits-yells

"Hey, do you know anything about skydiving?"

The other guy yells back, "No! But do you know anything about gas stoves?"

## Broken Radio

A film crew from the Hollywood, California was on location deep in the desert in Rajasthan. One day an Old Indian went up to the director and said, "Tomorrow rain." The next day it rained. A week later, the Indian went up to the director and said, "Tomorrow storm." The next day there was a hailstorm. "This Indian is incredible," said the director. He told his secretary to hire the Indian to predict the weather. However, after several successful predictions, the old Indian didn't show up for two weeks. Finally the director sent for him. "I have to shoot a big scene tomorrow," said the director, "and I'm depending on you. What will the weather be like?" The Indian shrugged his shoulders. "Don't know," he said. "My radio is broken."

## President's house

In 1978, I took my US born 4-year-old son to New Delhi to see historic sites. We reached the Indian President's house. I told my son, "ook this is the President's house."

My son looked at the magnificent building and said "Oh, Jimmy Carter lives here."

## A necktie

A country man moved to a big city and went to a night club that was notorious for having various kinds of troubles by the patrons. At the gate he was told that he needed to wear a tie. He went to his car, and the only thing he could find was a set of jumper cables. He tied them around his neck, and returned to the door of the nightclub. The manager stared at him and reluctantly said "OK, you can go in. But don't try to start anything."

## Hunting

The Game Warden stopped a deer hunter and asked to see his hunting license. "This is last year's license," the warden informed him.

"I know," said the hunter, "but I shouldn't need a new license, I am only shooting at the deer I missed last year."

## Moving

Approaching eighty-five years of age, Mrs. Narayanan finally decided it was time to give up her apartment in Mangalore and move to Mumbai. She was given the name of a Mumbai realtor, who enthusiastically drove her all over Mumbai, extolling the virtues of every apartment they looked at. "And this one, what a steal," he rhapsodized, "the investment of a lifetime. Why, in ten years it's gonna be worth three times..."

"Sorry," interrupted Mrs. Narayanan, "at my age I don't even buy green bananas."

## Mother calling

A man called his mother in Srinagar. He said to his mother, "How are you doing?" She said, "Not too good. I've been very weak."

The son then asked, "Why are you so weak?"

She said, "Because I haven't eaten in 38 days."

The son then asked, "How come you haven't eaten in 38 days?"

She said, "Because I didn't want my mouth to be filled with food when you called."

## Two ships

Did you hear about the red ship and the blue ship that collided?

-Both crews were marooned.

## A beggar

A beggar walks up to a well-dressed American woman who was visiting Varanasi,

"I haven't eaten anything in four days."

She looked at him and said, "God, I wish I had your willpower."